DUTCH ARCHITECTURE NEAR ALBANY
THE POLGREEN PHOTOGRAPHS

Dutch Architecture Near Albany
The Polgreen Photographs

SHIRLEY W. DUNN AND ALLISON P. BENNETT

PURPLE MOUNTAIN PRESS • FLEISCHMANNS, NEW YORK

Published by
Purple Mountain Press, Ltd.
Main Street, P.O. Box E3
Fleischmanns, New York 12330-0378
(914) 254-4062
FAX (914) 254-4476

First Edition

9 8 7 6 5 4 3 2 1

Library of Congress Cataloging-in-Publication Data

Dunn, Shirley W. (Shirley Wiltse), date
      Dutch architecture near Albany : the Polgreen photographs / Shirley W. Dunn and Allison P. Bennett.
        p.   cm.
      Includes bibliographical references and index.
      ISBN 0-935796-74-6 (pbk.)
        1. Architecture, Domestic—New York (State)—Albany Region—Pictorial works.   2. Architecture, Dutch—New York (State)—Albany Region—Pictorial works.   3. Architecture, Colonial—New York (State)—Albany Region—Pictorial works.   4. Architecture—New York (State)—Albany Region—Pictorial works.   5. Polgreen, Waldron Mosher, 1909–1944—Photograph collections.   I. Bennett, Allison Parker.   II. Title.
NA7235.N7D86 1996
728'.37'097474209033—dc20   96-16987
                                                 CIP

ISBN 0-935796-74-6

Manufactured in the United States of America

Cover: The Gerrit Staats House
Frontispiece: The Ariaantje Coeymans House

CONTENTS

ADDITIONAL ILLUSTRATIONS

ACKNOWLEDGMENTS

Many people have contributed to the preparation of this book. Roderic Blackburn gave valuable advice on the architectural text. Information sent by Jaap Schipper, an architect residing in Amsterdam, the Netherlands, has been very important. The interest and encouragement of Paul R. Huey, as well as his past help, also are greatly appreciated. Shelby Kriele gave welcome assistance with the Bronck House material, and Mark Peckham and Jaap Schipper contributed their unique drawings.

The authors express deepest thanks to Richard Polgreen for donating the negatives, and for sending photos and family information. A valuable letter containing information about Waldron Polgreen's life was received from Polgreen's surviving cousin, Sally Mosher McGinnis (Mrs. John McGinnis) of Westborough, Massachusetts.

The kind cooperation of publishers Wray and Loni Rominger was vital to the project. Among others who have made helpful contributions are Clarke Blair, Christopher Albright, Thomas Lanni, Gerald E. Dunn, Martha Slingerland, Katherine Herber, Eugene and Carol Parks, Shirley Mattice, Helen Strassner, Frank E. Martin, Betty W. Hannay, Paul and Brenda Winne, Fred and Kathleen Riester, Carl and Nancy Touhey, Mrs. David Kunz, Mary Krug, Connie and Barent Staats, Paul and Sylvia Lawler, Janet Nyquist, John Scharff, and Marc and Sarah Hafensteiner. The interest and assistance of staff at the Albany County Hall of Records is appreciated.

Waldron Mosher Polgreen, pictured about 1944

INTRODUCTION*

*Research on the life of Waldron Polgreen was done by Allison Bennett.

Presented here is a portfolio of photographs of Dutch colonial homes taken many years ago by Waldron Mosher Polgreen, a gentleman very much attuned to his own Dutch heritage. Some of these houses have been restored or renovated, others are being cared for by their owners, and some have disappeared from the landscape, ruined by neglect or torn down to make room for modern development. The coming years will probably see more of them lost. If so, they will be preserved only in written or visual records, as they are in Waldron Polgreen's photographs.

Waldron Mosher Polgreen was born June 22, 1909, and grew up in Albany. For years the family lived at 102 Willett Street, adjacent to Washington Park. Twin cousins, Sally and Emily Mosher, with whom he and his sister Edith played, lived next door at 100 Willett Street. The Polgreen family also resided at 239 South Main Avenue. Waldron, with his wife, Frances Dorn Polgreen, later lived in Albany at 101 Columbia Street and 130 Knox Street.

Polgreen attended the Albany Academy, and went to Hamilton College for a year before transferring to Northeastern University, from which he graduated. As an adult, he worked in the real estate and insurance office of his father, Henry W. Polgreen.

The Polgreens traced descent from the families of several Dutch settlers residing in the Albany area in the seventeenth century, including the Coeymans, Ten Eyck, Slingerland, Vandenbergh, Van Wie, Winne, Lansing, and Waldron families, as well as several others. Polgreen's mother, Grace Edith Mosher Polgreen, of Albany, was a charter member of the Dutch Settlers Society of Albany, founded in 1924, and also was active in other community organizations. (Membership in the Dutch Settlers Society, which she helped organize, is dependent on having proven ancestors who were living in the Albany environs before 1664, the date New Netherland was acquired by the English.)

Waldron Polgreen was the chairman of a Dutch Settlers Society committee that surveyed colonial buildings in the Albany area from 1936 to 1942. Some of the photographs in this book might have been taken for that survey; some were apparently taken before the survey began. Polgreen had an intense interest in the heritage of the Albany area. An article written by him about his ancestor, Tobias Ten Eyck, a sloop captain on the Hudson River, was printed in the 1944–45 issue of the *Dutch Settlers Society of Albany Yearbook*.

Polgreen was drafted into the army and served in the infantry during the Second World War. Tragically, he was killed in action on Christmas Day 1944, when his ship was torpedoed en route from England to France to deliver soldiers to the Battle of the Bulge. Polgreen was buried in the Cherbourg Military Cemetery in France. He left his parents, his wife, and three small sons—Richard Coeymans Polgreen, Henry Waldron Polgreen, and Tobias Ten Eyck Polgreen. A memorial stone for him was erected in the Polgreen plot in Albany Rural Cemetery. The family subsequently preserved Polgreen's favorite old desk, in which were stored his photographs and negatives.

According to his family, Waldron Polgreen had longed to live in the Albert Vanderzee House, owned by his mother's cousin. Raised in a family that treasured family mementos with Dutch connections, Polgreen felt a strong attraction to historic Dutch houses. The photographs, a lasting legacy, eloquently demonstrate his concern for the preservation of the houses associated with his Dutch heritage.

THE PHOTOGRAPHS

This detailed collection of black-and-white photographs of historic houses emerged from negatives preserved by Waldron Mosher Polgreen's family. These old negatives were presented to Shirley Dunn by Richard Polgreen, a son of the photographer; Allison Bennett was consulted to help identify the buildings. Shortly thereafter, the two historians made the decision to put the pictures in print.

Polgreen photographed houses in Albany, Rensselaer and Greene Counties. He had a box camera and used five-by-seven-inch sheet film; most negatives were on nitrate stock, though a few were safety film. His negatives were kept in some of the original Eastman film boxes, each of which originally held one dozen sheets. A few prints were kept in brown paper envelopes.

The pictures were taken in the 1930s and possibly very early 1940s. One envelope contains the words *by Waldron Polgreen 11 /4 /1933*. Four film boxes that originally contained unexposed film, in which Polgreen's negatives later were stored, carry expiration dates of 1934, 1935, 1937, and 1940. No other dates were recorded by the photographer, but a photo of the Vanderzee House is known to have been taken in 1934 or earlier.

Polgreen searched the area not far from Albany for houses of Dutch heritage, and photographed the exteriors. Often he took photos all the way around a building. Occasionally, however, the collection includes a negative only of the front (or, in one case, only of the back) of a structure. Much apparently depended upon his access to the property. In some cases, he visited a house in more than one season. Although it is possible more Polgreen photographs exist, no other repository of his pictures has been found.

He apparently had at hand a book still popular today, *Dutch Houses of the Hudson Valley before 1776*, by Helen Wilkinson Reynolds, published in 1929 by the Holland Society of New York. He may have used this book as a guide to find houses associated with Dutch ancestors. In a few cases, he positioned himself to duplicate the same views shown in Reynolds' book. However, Polgreen also photographed houses that Reynolds did not list.

THE ARCHITECTURAL CONTEXT

Polgreen's photographs provide an overview of eighteenth-century architecture in Albany, Rensselaer, and Greene Counties. Possibly by chance, perhaps knowingly, he included samples of building types that illustrate the evolution of Dutch-influenced construction from the early-eighteenth century, when North European forms were still part of the local vernacular, to the period after the Revolution, when the Dutch influence was waning.

The photographs provide an opportunity to present, in the text and captions that accompany them, information about the architectural specifics of the Dutch-influenced houses of the area. Little has been written on the subject. Although information on Dutch construction is available in a few books, no comprehensive guide to the architecture of the upper Hudson River's unique ethnic houses has been published.

Moreover, incorrect statements abound even in the scant literature about Dutch houses. Some editors of picture books of the 1930s and 1940s were unaware of the alterations and additions made to buildings over the years. Other writers assigned unreliable dates to old structures, or failed to note that the early appearance was entirely changed.

Today, understanding the gradual process of change, as well as finding accurate information about the structures, even those that survived into the twentieth century, is difficult. Travelers' descriptions of houses, written in earlier centuries, are generally superficial. Period paintings or drawings of seventeenth-century and early-eighteenth-century houses around or in Albany are rare; most representations of structures were done at a later date, after alterations had changed their appearance. Interiors are rarely shown. The few houses that have survived to the present have been modified or incorporated into larger structures, their original features obscured. Archeological digs to retrieve information about area houses have been valuable, but seldom occur.

Waldron Polgreen's photographs will be appreciated for providing illustrations of the unique Dutch-style houses with parapet gable-end walls and of the Dutch/English low gambrel-roofed houses, both of which characterized the area. His images are invaluable particularly because of the views of the sides and backs of houses. Although alterations have removed from surviving houses some of the early features described in the text, clues to their former existence can be sought in his pictures.

UNDERSTANDING
THE ARCHITECTURE*

W ALDRON POLGREEN photographed old houses in a large circle around Albany, New York. Each in some way was connected with his ancestors, most of them Dutch, or with the area's Dutch heritage. His interest was not unique. In every era, the special character of the "Dutch" houses associated with the first settlers of New York has intrigued observers.

The late-seventeenth- and early-eighteenth-century houses in the Hudson Valley built by descendants of North European settlers were distinctive for their resemblance to foreign structures. The houses were different from their New England and southern counterparts, and formed a recognizable regional architecture. The architectural antecedents of the houses extend back to the arrival of Dutch colonists in the mid-seventeenth century. Travelers frequently noted the connections between the houses they saw and the origins of the population. As late as 1796, a visitor noted of Albany, "In the old part of the town the streets are very narrow, and the houses are frightful; they are all built in the old Dutch taste."[1]

A notable exterior element that caught the eye of strangers was the wall rising above the roof on one or both gable ends. A correspondent for an English magazine noted of Albany in 1789, "The houses . . . are built in the old Low Dutch style, with the gable-ends toward the street, and terminating at the top with a kind of parapet, indented like stairs."[2]

The houses with gable-end walls that formed low parapets were especially popular in the upper Hudson Valley from the last third of the seventeenth century, when brick became widely available, through the 1740s. In the countryside, however, judging from surviving examples, the parapet walls lacked the stair-like indentations once popular in Albany.

*This chapter on Dutch construction is by Shirley Dunn.

1. Joel Munsell, ed., *The Annals of Albany*, 10 vols. (Albany: Joel Munsell, 1850–1859), 1:154.

2. *The Columbian Magazine* (December, 1789), no page. This English publication can be found at the Albany Institute of History and Art, McKinney Library.

1.1: The gable-end wall of the Leendert Bronck House (page 67), rises above the roof at each end. A loft door at the top of the gable retains Dutch-style hinges. Settling at the corners is indicated by mortar repairs, which also outline the Dutch cross bond brick pattern.

Despite similarities to houses in the Netherlands, the early houses of the Hudson Valley and other areas of Dutch and North European settlement were adaptations, rather than exact counterparts, of the residences left behind. Materials, climate, and especially soil conditions in the Dutch colony on the Hudson, differed from those in the Netherlands. The pattern of land leasing in the Hudson Valley also affected house size and style.

TIES TO OLD WORLD ARCHITECTURE

After the final English acquisition of the Dutch colony in 1674, trade with the Netherlands was restricted. Family contacts and the Dutch Reformed Church, led by Dutch-speaking ministers from the Netherlands, maintained loose cultural ties between the Dutch enclave in New York and the Netherlands. The Dutch in the Hudson Valley retained archaic customs, spoke a colloquial form of their language, and built unique houses for almost a century after the English takeover. Individuals from the Albany area who went to New York for trade, and for social or political reasons, learned to speak to and mingle with the English population and to wear English-style clothes; nevertheless, they retained their religion, traditions and language at home.

As a result, the reflection in local houses of European styles from a century earlier was apparent well into the eighteenth century. As the halfway mark of that century passed, however, Dutch-influenced housing in the Hudson Valley changed with the times. New houses were built and older houses were enlarged and modernized. Residents here, isolated from direct visual influences from the Netherlands, were drawn instead by local trends and by new American styles.

Some information about the construction of early Dutch-style houses in the Albany area is given in building contracts found in the Van Rensselaer family papers and in Albany County records of the latter half of the seventeenth century. Most of the contracts originally were written in Dutch; they are subject to the difficulties of translation from an archaic language.

The houses described in these contracts were small by today's standards. A house built on the east shore of the Hudson a few miles south of Albany in 1678 was to be "at least the length of a board square."[3] This was about fifteen feet by fifteen feet in the measure of the day, possibly even smaller by modern

3. A.J.F. van Laer, ed., and Jonathan Pearson, trans., *Early Records of the City and County of Albany and Colony of Rensselaerswyck*, 4 vols. (Albany: Joel Munsell, and The University of the State of New York, 1869–1919), 3:459.

measurements. The barn intended to accompany the house was to be larger—some thirty feet long and twenty-eight feet broad.

In Dutch measure, one foot (a wood foot) was equivalent to slightly over eleven inches by today's measure. However, in the 1670s, either Dutch or a variant of English measure might be used, leading to some uncertainty about the exact length of the measurements given in the contracts.[4]

Haphazard houses, it was believed, detracted from the order and safety of urban areas. By 1676, an Albany ordinance required houses within the city to be "substantial dwelling houses" not less than eighteen feet wide, and at least two rooms deep. To improve the city's appearance, the houses were to have brick or quarrystone fronts on the end facing the street, and, for fire safety, tiled roofs.[5]

The ordinance was effective. As the city was built up, brick facades proved the popular choice. Because of the brick fronts, some eighteenth-century visitors erroneously thought the houses of Albany were made of brick. However, the hidden part of the house usually was frame, covered with horizontal boards on the sides.

Old pantile roofs lingered in Albany into the nineteenth century. As late as 1838, a house at the northeast corner of Pearl and Steuben Streets was described as "a Dutch burgher's residence, bearing the date of 1732, its yellow and ill-cemented bricks, its small windows and doors, its low body and immensely disproportioned sloping roof, covered with tiles of all shapes and fashions, shewing what description of city Albany was likely to have been a century ago."[6] Traditional roof tiles often were imported from the Netherlands. The ones made locally were not satisfactory, according to Peter Kalm, a visitor in 1749.[7]

COUNTRY HOUSES

Although country farmhouses were not affected by lot dimensions or city ordinances, patterns of landholding influenced house size outside the city of Albany. Most mid- to late-seventeenth-century rural houses around Albany were on the farms of Rensselaerswyck, the territory controlled by the Van Rensselaer family. The directors of Rensselaerswyck usually provided a small tenant house as well as a barn, hay barrack and fences for each farm. While

4. The length of a *board*—fifteen English feet—was mandated by an order of 1676. See van Laer, *Minutes of the Court of Albany, Rensselaerswyck and Schenectady 1675–1680* (Albany: University of the State of New York, 1928), 109. For the length of a Dutch *wood foot* (11.15 inches English), see *Early Records of the City and County of Albany and Colony of Rensselaerswyck*, 1:5.

5. A.J.F. van Laer, ed. and trans., *Minutes of the Court of Albany, Rensselaerswyck and Schenectady, 1675–1680* (Albany: University of the State of New York, 1928), 136.

6. James Silk Buckingham, "The Fourth of July, 1838," in Roger Haydon, ed., *Upstate Travels, British Views of Nineteenth-Century New York* (Syracuse: Syracuse University Press, 1982), 71.

7. Peter Kalm, *Peter Kalm's Travels in North America: The English Version*, ed. Adolph B. Benson, 2 vols. (New York: Dover, 1966), 1:341.

the structures could vary according to the agreement with the tenant, the crowding of family and servants into a single house was expected. Subdividing a farm was prohibited, and building an additional house for a son's or daughter's family on rented property also was forbidden. Thus, a farm residence usually was not a reflection of the architecture of the tenant family's area of origin in the Netherlands. Modest farmhouses in the Netherlands, familiar to the Patroon and successive directors of Rensselaerswyck, were models for the tenant houses of Rensselaerswyck.

Seventeenth-century speculators, such as Gerrit Teunis Van Vechten and Marte Gerritse Van Bergen (Van Rensselaer farmers who later bought lands beyond Rensselaerswyck), rented farms to their own tenants on terms modeled on the leases of Rensselaerswyck. Anxious for profits, they were frugal landlords who supplied to their tenants small houses similar to those of Rensselaerswyck. Although inducements sometimes had to be offered to lure tenants to remote farms, these inducements were usually offers of postponement of rent or promises of future use of additional land rather than better housing.

The area-wide pattern of farms rented with three- to five-year contracts led to a minimum standard in the housing provided; in addition, the short leases limited the tenants' willingness to invest in alterations and improvements.

A 1682 contract gives an example of late-seventeenth-century country style in Rensselaerswyck. Claes Van Petten, who was renting a farm along the Hudson River south of the present city of Rensselaer, was to have a new brick house, as agreed when he signed his 1680 lease. Van Petten's house was contracted for by Maria Van Rensselaer, who was managing Rensselaerswyck. Van Rensselaer had agreed to allow him to take the farm, although she was annoyed with the previous tenant, Gerrit Teunis Van Vechten, for cutting short his lease.[8]

The house ordered by Van Rensselaer for Van Petten was to be twenty-two and one-half feet square (possibly closer to twenty feet square by today's measurements). The house was to have one floor seven and one-half feet high (the cellar); a second floor (the living floor) was to be eight feet high. The house wall was to extend two feet above the attic floor level, forming the half story which became the garret. Pantiles were to cover the roof, indicating the house had gable-end parapet walls, and the structure was to be finished with doors and windows.[9]

8. Maria Van Rensselaer, *Correspondence of Maria Van Rensselaer*, ed. and trans. A.J.F. van Laer (Albany: University of the State of New York, 1935), 39.

9. New York State Library, Manuscripts and Special Collections, Van Rensselaer Papers, Item 11408.

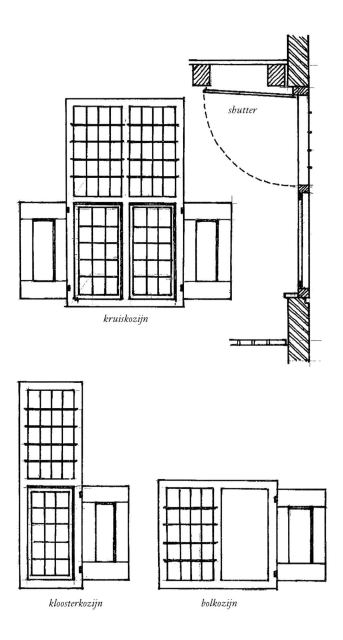

shutter

kruiskozijn

kloosterkozijn   *bolkozijn*

1.2: The types of windows specified in late-seventeenth-century Albany area building contracts. Drawing by Dutch architect Jaap Schipper, 1995.

This house was more substantial than most, because it was on an established farm which was considered one of the best in Rensselaerswyck and Van Petten was a tenant of substance. A house built nearby on a less-profitable farm in 1678 was less than half as large.

A frame farmhouse built in 1681 on a farm about a mile away from Claes Van Petten also was detailed in a contract. It was to be "twenty-five feet long by twenty-two feet wide." Under it there was to be a cellar hole fifteen feet square, sheathed with oak slabs.[10] A house with such an interior storage cellar rested either on a stone foundation or on wooden piers. The piers may have been the corner posts of the house, set in the ground, as was done in wet areas of the Netherlands, where cellars were not possible.[11]

Cool but frost-free cellars, needed for the vital storage of fruit and vegetable crops in the cold Hudson Valley, gradually became larger. By the end of the seventeenth century, full cellars with stone sidewalls were the norm. One house built in 1725 was described as having two cellars, "a summer cellar and underneath a winter cellar, in which it never freezes."[12]

Other early building contracts specified the fittings of houses, particularly the casement windows opening into the house. Three kinds of window openings were mentioned. The *bolkozijn* was two side-by-side rectangles, one or both sides containing leaded glass panes in a hinged sash, with one or both sides covered by an outside shutter. Other windows were variations of the first: A *kruiskozijn* was a four-section unit divided by mullions, with stationary glass sections at the top and shutters in combination with casement windows on the bottom; a *kloosterkozijn* was the left or right half of a *kruiskozijn*. In the Netherlands, the fixed glass had an inside shutter.

In addition to windows, built-in bedsteads, stairs to the garret, and wooden roofs sometimes were itemized in the building agreements. A contract of 1676 for a house in present-day Columbia County specified a structure twenty feet square, with "two casement windows . . . a door frame, a cloister window frame . . . together with a back door, two end bents with corbels, a cellar to be boarded up, to lay a floor therein [the cellar] 20 feet in breadth and 15 feet long, cellar stairs and stairs to the garret, to make the doors as well of the cellar as of the house, to cut to the right length and dress the boards both of the floor and the garret, to hang the windows and doors, to make the wooden hinges to the doors." The contractor was to "suitably cover the roof of the

10. *Early Records of the City and County of Albany and Colony of Rensselaerswyck*, 3:516.

11. Correspondence May 5, 1986, of Henk Zantkuyl, an engineer with the Municipal Office for Preservation and Restoration of Buildings, Amsterdam, the Netherlands, with Paul R. Huey.

12. *The Papers of Sir William Johnson*, 14 vols. (Albany, N.Y. 1921), 1:203.

13. Pearson and van Laer, *Early Records of the City and County of Albany and Colony of Rensselaerswyck*, 3:346. Translation corrected by Dr. Charles Gehring.

14. *Peter Kalm's Travels in North America*, 2:612; Shirley Dunn, "The Plank Roof: *met planken bequaem decken*," *Dutch Barn Preservation Society Newsletter*, 3:2 (fall, 1990): 3,4. The term in Dutch contracts was usually *planken*, which should be translated "planks"; however, the terms "planks" and "boards" have been used interchangeably by some translators. Peter Kalm's original diary was in Swedish. Because the English version was made from a revised German translation, some fine distinctions may have been lost.

15. In the 1930s, some surviving examples of characteristic country houses, with gable-end parapet walls or later gambrel roofs, were photographed by Polgreen. Most of the houses he recorded were made of brick. Therefore, the text, which is based on his selections, emphasizes brick houses of both architectural types.

house with planks." All this and two square hay barracks were to be produced for twenty beaver skins.[13]

Boards (often called *planks* in early contracts) were commonly used for roofs on houses and barns in the seventeenth and eighteenth centuries, according to early building contracts and later travelers' accounts. In 1749, Peter Kalm, describing how the houses belonging to the Dutch in the country near Albany were built, noted that their roofs were made either of boards or shingles.[14] Some of these roofs, made of fitted horizontal boards with chamfered edges, have survived under later coverings of shingles. (See the photograph of the Gerrit Vandenbergh House, page 15.)

As the building contracts and other sources make clear, many houses were made of wood. Only a few wooden houses from the seventeenth and early-eighteenth centuries have survived in the upper Hudson Valley, however; brick or stone houses survived in larger numbers.[15]

EFFECTS OF LONG-TERM LEASES

The housing situation changed on the farms outside of Albany toward the end of the seventeenth century, as "perpetual" leases began to be sold by the Van Rensselaers. A lessee who "bought" a long-term farm lease was responsible for his own taxes and his own housing. Although not truly an owner (leases required yearly payments of tithes and communal work contributions), the structures he built were his. Such a lessee appeared on lists of freeholders, and he and his family considered the farm their property. He could build a house which reflected his own needs and tastes rather than those of a landlord. The freeholder was, of course, still imbued with the conservative Dutch traditions of the area, and worked within the limitations of traditional style, available building materials, and his often limited means.

Another effect of the leasing change was that farms could now be divided among sons. If there were no sons, sections of a farm frequently were offered to daughters and their husbands. As the old tenant houses were replaced or new houses were added to farms from 1690 to 1740, a recognizable housing style emerged. Steep roofs, jambless fireplaces, casement windows, divided exterior doors, full stone cellars and a wood frame were the norm. The use of bricks laid over the wood frame was popular because the walls lasted well and

1.3: Under the shingles of this section of the Gerrit Vandenbergh House (page 58) is an old roof made of chamfered boards.

resisted fire. Stone was used for walls where it was abundant; frame houses were also built. The new houses echoed materials, framing, windows, hardware, fireplaces and other architectural elements common to their predecessors, but, with two rooms on the first floor, they were longer than the earlier tenant houses.

Early in the eighteenth century, larger bricks began to be used, in accordance with a 1703 New York colonial law requiring bricks to be 9 by 4.25 by 2.5 inches.[16] Interestingly, most bricks in surviving houses are not the exact size required by the law. For example, a sample brick from the Van Wie House of 1732 is 9 by 4.375 by 2 inches, while a brick from the Van Rensselaer-Genet House site of 1753 is 9 by 4.625 by 2.25 inches. Bricks from the Gerrit Staats House range from 8.5 to 9.5 inches in length. Prior to 1703, bricks had been closer in size to Dutch models, which were thinner and shorter.[17]

DEFINING DUTCH STYLE IN HOUSES NEAR ALBANY

Two full generations resident in this country separated the builders of houses near Albany in the early-eighteenth century from the area's seventeenth-century Dutch settlers. Most of the new builders had never seen an old Dutch house in the Netherlands, so they could not duplicate European houses. Instead, local Dutch housing traditions controlled design. Consequently, although houses had many variations, builders copied from the town and country residences of respected family members, as well as from other existing structures in the Albany area.

Houses of the eighteenth century modestly reflected their owners' status and success. Located on private farms with perpetual leases, the houses were long-term homesteads of families whose members included not only farmers but lawyers, elected officials, merchants, sloop captains, innkeepers, and blacksmiths and other artisans. The owners were members of the extensive family networks that characterized their society. Most were churchgoers who regularly went to Albany, Kinderhook or Leeds to attend the Dutch Reformed Church; a few were Lutherans. Members of these families were leaders in the regional economic expansion which gradually made the area more cosmopolitan.

Thus, for the most part, the rural and urban houses of the busy society of the first half of the eighteenth century were decades removed from prototypes

16. *The Colonial Laws of New York from the Year 1664 to the Revolution*, (Albany: James B. Lyon, State Printer, 1896), 556.

17. The Van Wie measurement is from a March 1995 letter from John Stevens to Shirley Dunn. For a discussion of brick size, see Roderic H. Blackburn and Ruth Piwonka, *Remembrance of Patria: Dutch Arts and Culture in Colonial America, 1609-1776*, (Albany Institute of History and Art, 1988), 127.

in the Netherlands. They were, nevertheless, the foreign-looking houses of the upper Hudson Valley region that gave the area its Dutch flavor in the eyes of outsiders and visitors.

The "Dutch-style" house of the late-seventeenth and early-eighteenth centuries retained features described in the building contracts quoted above. (Later, mid-eighteenth-century gambrel-roofed houses reflected some English influences.) The Dutch influence can be identified and defined by the framing and by traditional elements such as roof line, hardware, brick bond, fireplaces, and windows. A checklist of some of the architectural features of the brick country residences built in the traditional Dutch style popular in the first half of the eighteenth century around Albany might include the following:

Exterior

Steep roofs, with gable-end parapet walls (brick walls extending above the roof line about four to six inches). These gable walls had either pinnacles of brick at each end or end chimneys. The Hendrick Van Wie and Leendert Bronck Houses were good examples.

Vlechtingen (literally braided brick sections, also called brick tumbling), inverted triangles of brick along the slope of the gable. By turning the bricks, the builder avoided cutting them and presented the hardened shells of the bricks to the weather to prevent water penetration. (See the Van Wie and Leendert Bronck Houses.)

Loft openings that gave light, access and air circulation to two levels of garret (attic) storage. One or both levels of the garret had rectangular, shuttered openings; on one end, the higher garret level usually also had ventilating holes built into the bricks.

Casement windows that opened into the house, with lead strips holding small rectangular or diamond-shape pieces of glass. Over time, lead strips gave way to wooden muntins, holding rectangular glass panes.[18] Few leaded windows have survived; most were destroyed during the American Revolution, when lead was requisitioned for bullets. (See the old painting of the Ariaantje Coeymans House, page 40, for examples of Dutch-style windows.) Frames for casement windows were preserved on the Slingerland and Van Wie Houses.

Shutters, brightly painted on the inside.

18. The grooved strips of lead are not properly called "cames," since this refers to cast lead at an earlier stage of manufacture. See Isabel Davies, "Window glass in Eighteenth-Century Williamsburg," in *Five Artifact Studies*, Colonial Williamsburg Foundation (Virginia, 1973): 82. For a good illustration of a casement window with wooden muntins, see W. Max Reid, *The Mohawk Valley* (New York: G.P. Putnam's Sons, 1901), 169.

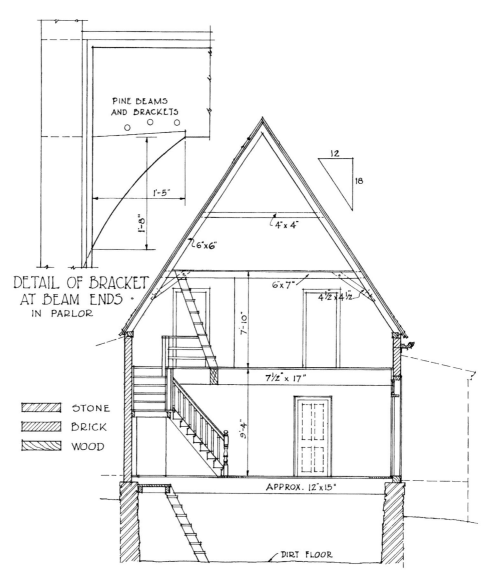

PINE BEAMS
AND BRACKETS

1'-5"

1'-8"

DETAIL OF BRACKET
AT BEAM ENDS
IN PARLOR

6"x6"

4"x 4"

12
18

6"x 7"

4½"x4½"

7'-10"

STONE
BRICK
WOOD

7½" x 17"

9'-4"

APPROX. 12"x15"

DIRT FLOOR

1.4: This cross-section of the Hendrick Bries House, from the 1934 Historic American Buildings Survey, includes the stair and shows the two levels of storage in the garret. Also depicted is a corbel (here called a bracket) with its curved soffit, typical of those that originally supported the deep, seventeen-inch by seven and one-half-inch beams of the first floor. In 1934, the corbels could be seen in the parlor, but not in the kitchen. Such braces, which protruded into the room, were often removed in the nineteenth century when owners tried to modernize with plaster ceilings.

1.5: The steep roof angle of the Hendrick Bries House (page 47) is found in other area Dutch-style brick houses of the early 1700s. *Vlechtingen*—the triangles of brick inserted along the incline of the gable parapet walls—make a smooth, water-resistant edge along the surface. The Dutch cross brick bond is clear. Wall anchors close to the end of the building are attached to the vertical timber posts within each corner. The windows shown are not original.

Hinges of wrought iron, with round or oval nailing pads, and with spade-shaped points on the ends. Rarely, the end points were divided into two curves or took other forms.

A front door located off-center on the facade; occasionally there was a door directly into each room.

A transom window (four or five panes set into a frame) over the front door. (Note, for example, the Van Wie House, page 54).

Brick walls, laid in Dutch cross bond around a timber frame (as in the Hendrick Bries House). The vertical posts of the timber frame were visible in the plastered interior rooms, but were covered with bricks on the exterior; the presence of the frame was revealed by exterior wall anchors close to the corners. The Dutch cross bond resulted in a diamond pattern on the walls; sometimes the pattern was emphasized by blackened brick headers. This pattern was an old Dutch tradition; in the Netherlands it was believed that the diamond pattern warded off evil.[19]

19. August 1986 letter to Paul R. Huey from Jan Baart, head of the Archeological Division of the Department of Public Works, Amsterdam and the Amsterdam Historical Museum.

Interior

A first-floor plan of two rooms, sometimes with an entrance foyer or reception space. There were no closets; heavy furniture pieces were used for storage.

Vertical wall posts, spaced about four feet apart, supporting heavy horizontal ceiling joists, commonly called beams. The posts continued above the beams for two to four feet to the wall plate, on which the roof rafters rested.

Braces (corbels) with curved soffits, strengthening the connection of some or all of the wall posts with the beams. (See the HABS drawing of the Bries House, page 18.)

Beams (joists) above the first floor, regularly spaced, uniform except for a larger beam needed to carry the extra weight of the brick chimney. The first-floor beams were smoothly finished and sometimes decorated with beaded edges, as they were intended to be exposed. The boards of the floor above formed the ceiling.

Jambless (hanging) fireplaces in the first-floor rooms. These open fireplaces had no sides or only decorative jambs, and were backed by a brick or other fireproof wall. An iron fireback protected the brick wall. (Visitors to New York City and to the Albany area noted these fireplaces, which were very different from the ones in New England.) The tapered chimney stack of the

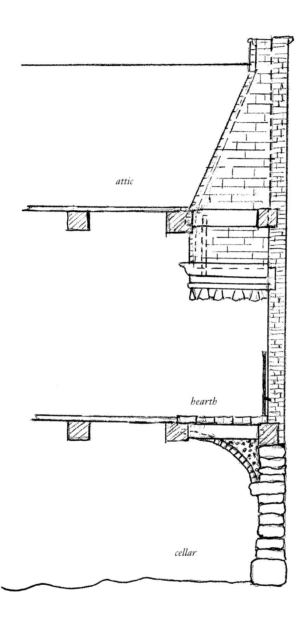

attic

hearth

cellar

1.6: A side view of a jambless fireplace shows the chimney rising above the smoke hood over the fireplace. The arch below the hearth rests on a projecting stone built into the cellar wall. Drawing by Shirley Dunn.

jambless fireplace was supported above the first floor. Below the chimney, a smoke hood (commonly plastered and lined with bricks) was supported by a timber frame projecting from the brick wall and by iron straps or wooden hangers. Trimmed with crown molding and faced with a board, the hood also was edged with cloth to catch the smoke. The resulting fireplaces, according to one visitor, had the appearance of canopy beds.[20] Such fireplaces were popular for cooking because the cook could use either a hot fire in the center, or coals in several locations. They also were pleasant to sit beside, and the Dutch hated to give them up. The fireplace did not have an oven—baking was done in covered utensils over the coals on the hearth. Some houses had ovens in kitchen outbuildings or wings; according to tradition, the Hendrick Van Wie House once had a stone building nearby for slaves' quarters and cooking.[21]

An arch of brick in the cellar, or an angled cradle (support) of boards, reaching from a horizontal stone placed in the cellar wall to the first joist. This arch supported the hearth of the first-floor fireplace.

Cellar joists made of hewn timbers, a foot or more deep, spanning the cellar from wall to wall, with no intervening framing for a hall.

A small, space-saving staircase on the first floor, often enclosed, leading to the garret.

An unfinished, unheated garret with a board floor, and with an upper loft level, often partly floored. One garret was described in a letter as "a garret, 40 feet long and 24 feet wide all through, and a garret-loft; on which two garrets some thousands of schepels [of grain] can be stored."[22]

Generally, only the first floor of these story-and-a-half houses was the living area. In wood-frame houses, wall fillings of wattle and daub (mud and straw mixed, placed around oak strips or pointed saplings) or of soft bricks were placed between the vertical posts on the outer wall, under the clapboards, to keep the living rooms warmer. Sometimes an enclosed bed was built in the warm first-floor area.

Because the unheated garret and the garret loft were intended for storage, an outside loft door was commonly installed in one gable wall or, more rarely, in a large dormer in the roof front (see the Ariaantje Coeymans House, page 38). The loft door might be topped by a crane and pulley, so that bulky barrels and

20. *Columbian Magazine,* December, 1789, no page.

21. Helen Wilkinson Reynolds, *Dutch Houses in the Hudson Valley before 1776,* (1929; reprinted New York: Dover Publications, 1965), 124.

22. *The Papers of Sir William Johnson,* 1:203.

bags could be lifted up for storage inside. (Other ingenious arrangements were used for access to the garret; see the Van Wie House, page 57, for an example.)

The tapering chimney rose from the first-floor ceiling, through the garret, to an exit at the ridge, either at the gable end or in the center of the house. There was no ridgepole in the garret—rafter pairs were joined at the peak and pegged.

Dates or initials in wrought iron, or on incised tiles or stones, fixed in the brick, were common. However, these sometimes were added at a later date, and may refer to renovations as well as to original construction.

A special type of barn was part of the rural setting of Dutch-style houses. It had a steep roof, low sidewalls, and double doors in the gable ends. On the inside, an aisled frame featured large anchor beams over a center threshing floor. Barns of this type accompanied the later gambrel-roofed houses as well. The recognizable "Dutch" barn, with its companion hay barrack (a stack for hay or grain with a movable thatched roof supported on poles), contributed to the distinctive scene that reminded travelers they were in a country settled by the Dutch. Dutch barns and hay barracks were once present near many of the houses documented in Polgreen's photographs.

As the eighteenth century progressed, houses changed, even in the conservative Dutch areas. Outside influences filtered into the Dutch strongholds. The first half of the eighteenth century saw an influx of immigrants. Many Germans from the Palatinate, who had made stops in the Netherlands and often spoke Dutch, moved into the Hudson Valley. After their original settlement failed, the Palatine settlers and subsequent Protestant arrivals spread out and intermarried with the Dutch population. Later, the outbreak of two wars with French Canada brought soldiers and traders of several nationalities, particularly English and Scots, to the area. Some of these outsiders also married into local Dutch families and settled here, especially after 1755. New Englanders in large numbers began to arrive in the 1760s.

HOUSING TRENDS

By the middle of the eighteenth century, new architectural styles became popular along the Hudson. One style featured a story-and-a-half house constructed with a gambrel roof. A sprinkling of gambrels had appeared in previous decades, but in the area around Albany the style did not gain momentum until the 1750s.

The gambrel-roof style houses that became popular in the Albany area along the Hudson River had no prototype in the Netherlands, and they also broke with the earlier Dutch-style houses in floor plan and framing. The rural story-and-a-half gambrel-roofed examples, such as the Van Rensselaer-Genet and Gerrit Staats Houses, nevertheless retained many Dutch-style features typical of the Hudson Valley, such as loft doors and the Dutch cross bond. Transitional brick gambrels were built with timber frames under the bricks, and the earlier gambrels, on their lower roofs, copied the pitch of Dutch-style roofs. Moreover, the hardware changed little.

Not surprisingly, then, despite its English-style roof and its Georgian-influenced central hall plan, the gambrel-roofed house is commonly described as "Dutch." Aside from the architectural connections, the term reflects the ancestry of the owners and the traditions of the areas where the gambrels were built. Indeed, the gambrel-roofed story-and-a-half houses outside of Albany were built generally on farms located within a mile of the Hudson River. They were occupied by descendants of families that had been part of the early settlement of the Dutch colony. The De Freests, Schermerhorns, Van Deusens, Ten Eycks, Van Schaicks, Wendells, Staats, Lansings, Witbecks, Van der Heydens, Van Rensselaers and others—all prosperous descendants of early arrivals— were among those who erected area gambrel-roofed country houses in the mid- to late-eighteenth century.[23]

23. Taller, two-story houses with gambrel roofs, central halls, and Palladian details were popular choices among merchants arriving from New England and New York in the 1770s and 1780s.

Despite traditional details, gambrels reflected new trends in the way Hudson Valley Dutch families used space and heat. A large room, with a smaller room behind it, opening on each side of a first-floor hall, became a common floor plan. Jambless fireplaces and casement windows gradually disappeared, supplanted by windows with double-hung sash and by jambed fireplaces of English derivation. A bedroom, heated by its own fireplace, soon appeared on one end of the second floor. The rest of the attic, however, continued to be used as unheated storage space, in the older way. Many houses were not fully finished upstairs until mid-nineteenth-century remodelings occurred.

In gambrel-roofed houses, the wide first-floor hall extending through the house became important as a reception and sitting area. One observer noted

1.7: The gambrel-roofed Van Rensselaer-Genet House (page 77) viewed from the southwest. Wall anchors near the corners indicate the brick is laid around a wooden frame, as in the earlier Dutch-style houses. The original front-window openings, which had lintels of vertical bricks, remain. The windows shown are replacements.

24. Anne [McVicar] Grant,
*Memoirs of an American Lady:
With Sketches of Manners and
Scenes in America As They
Existed Previous to The
Revolution; With Unpublished
Letters and a Memoir of Mrs.
Grant, by James Grant Wilson*
(1901; reprinted Freeport,
N.Y.: Books for Libraries
Press, 1972), 165, 166.

that with the front and rear doors open, in summer the hall was the coolest place in the house, and consequently the family congregated there.[24] The hall was not usually located precisely in the middle of the house in early examples of gambrels—reflecting the Dutch lack of concern for symmetry. Consequently, some front doors, such as that of the Tobias Ten Eyck House, were off-center, as in earlier houses. The front door moved more nearly to the center in later examples of the gambrel-roofed house, as Georgian-style balance became more important.

Underneath the gambrel-roofed house, joists stretching across the width of the cellar were interrupted for cross-framing under the hall. The bedroom level of the gambrel-roof style was reached by a broad stairway, often with a landing, which occupied a substantial place in the hall. First-floor rooms were more specialized and more decorative than in older Dutch-style houses; cabinets were built on the walls beside the jambed fireplaces. Paneling, such as in the Tobias Ten Eyck House, flourished over mantels, on cabinet walls, on doors, and on hall wainscoting.

First-floor fireplaces in gambrel-roofed houses were located inside gable ends. Although some early gambrel-roofed houses featured a jambless fireplace at each end,[25] and the c.1760 transitional Tobias Ten Eyck House had a jambless fireplace at one end and a jambed fireplace at the other, many gambrel-roofed houses featured English-style fireplaces with jambs (brick sides). The design of the jambed fireplace required a substantial cellar support of brick or stone piers, in contrast to the minimal hearth support of a Dutch-style jambless fireplace.

25. Examples are two Defreest
Houses in Defreestville, and a
Schermerhorn House in
Schodack Landing. Both
communities are in
Rensselaer County.

Most gambrel-roofed houses retained a divided Dutch-style entrance door (albeit paneled and with diagonal backing), hung with traditional Dutch hinges. Plaster ceilings gradually became common, and the now-smaller first-floor beams were hidden. Double-hung windows appeared on the public faces of the living areas of houses.

Although brick gambrel-roofed houses usually retained a hidden timber frame, a few had load-bearing brick walls. Dutch cross bond, and occasionally Flemish bond (a bond with alternating headers and stretchers), were used for the brickwork; common bond appeared on the rear and side walls. *Vlechtingen* along the roof slope were no longer needed, since the top of the wall was covered by the roof.

Gambrel-roofed houses were popular until the 1790s. By early in the nineteenth century, however, any "Dutch look" had become totally old fashioned, and old Dutch-style houses with steep roofs (and even not-so-old gambrel-roofed houses) were frequently remodeled or replaced.

Polgreen photographed a selection both of the old Dutch-style houses with parapet gable ends and the later gambrel-roofed "Dutch" houses. In addition, he ferreted out another type of house occupied by some of his ancestors—a gable-roofed house, of New England influence, built with a center hall and jambed fireplaces, and adorned with Federal-style moldings and trim. Examples are the Moak-Leedings and Slingerland-Winne Houses. Such houses, built of wood, brick, or stone, had floor plans similar to those of gambrel-roofed houses.

The gable-roofed houses, often built by latecomers to the area, frequently featured a divided Dutch-style door, and today are referred to as "Dutch" because of their age and the area's Dutch heritage. In reality, they had little architectural connection to the regional Dutch-style houses pre-dating the 1750s.

In the city of Albany, where new, taller structures made more efficient use of limited lot space than the seventeenth- and eighteenth-century houses, the old Dutch houses were gradually removed. In the countryside, where more houses survived, some were given Greek Revival trim and windows, and finished off upstairs. Others were "Victorianized" as the nineteenth century progressed. Having survived two centuries, a number of significant early houses were lost in the Albany area during the depression years of the 1930s and early 1940s, as Polgreen's photographs attest.

OPPOSITE PAGE: A segment of *Map of the Manor Renselaerwick* [*sic*], prepared in 1767 by surveyor John R. Bleeker, identifies houses existing at the time.

Locations shown on the east side of the Hudson River, which divides the map horizontally, include:
 Van Rensselaer-Genet House, 39
 Hendrick Bries House, 40
 Joachim Staats and Gerrit Staats Houses, Letter B.

Houses identified on the west side of the river are:
 Ariaantje Coeymans House, 2
 Hendrick Van Wie House, 6
 Gerrit Vandenbergh House, 11
 Teunis Slingerland House, 120
 Van Sante-Bleecker House, 121
 Harmen Vanderzee House, 122
 Tobias Ten Eyck House, 135.

The map is found in E.B. O'Callaghan, *The Documentary History of the State of New York*, vol. 3 (Albany, 1850).

The key below shows the approximate location of the section of the Bleeker map shown.

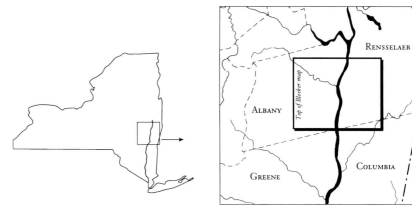

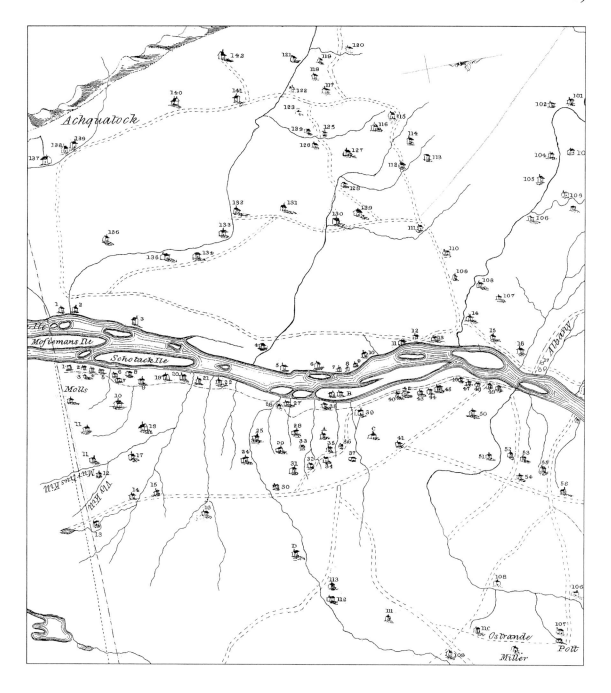

2.1: The south facade (once the back of the house) of the Joachim Staats House is perpendicular to the Hudson River, at left. The frame addition on the west end was added about 1880. The slope of the ground leads to a knoll, the *hooge berg*, behind the house.

TWO EARLY STONE DUTCH-STYLE HOUSES

THE JOACHIM STAATS HOUSE

Location: The Joachim Staats House is at the south end of Papscanee Island, also called Staats Island, in Schodack, Rensselaer County. Papscanee Island is on the east side of the Hudson River, south of the city of Rensselaer.

History: This stone house on Papscanee Island was occupied late in the seventeenth century by Joachim Staats and his wife, Anna Barentse Reynders. It was erected on a parcel which jestingly had been christened the *hooge berg* (high hill) farm by a previous owner, Gysbert Cornelise (Vandenbergh), whose farmhouse burned in 1679.[1] The location of the Vandenbergh house and its replacement, if any, is unknown. Probably to avoid recurrent floods, the Staats House was built halfway up the *hooge berg*, the highest point on flat Papscanee Island.

Joachim Staats, an attorney, obtained a deed for the farm from Kiliaen Van Rensselaer, patroon of Rensselaerswyck, in 1696. Joachim possibly had hoped for a farm across the river on Marte Gerritsen's Island (Castle Island), below Albany. Joachim's brother, Samuel Staats, a surgeon who lived in New York, had tried to buy Marte Gerritsen's Island from the Van Rensselaers in Holland as early as 1688. However, the branch of the Van Rensselaer family at Albany refused to give up that valuable island; instead, Samuel Staats, Joachim Staats, and a co-participant, Barent Reynders, a sailmaker from New York, later received two farms on Papscanee Island and one on the east-side mainland nearby.[2]

Joachim Staats may have been living on his Papscanee Island site before the 1696 deed was issued, while awaiting the final agreements. It was reported in

1. *Correspondence of Maria Van Rensselaer,* 27.

2. Shirley W. Dunn, "Settlement Patterns in Rensselaerswijck: Tracing the *Hooge Berg,* a Seventeenth Century Farm on the East Side of the Hudson" in *de Halve Maen,* vol. lxviii (spring 1995): 18, 19.

3. Joel Munsell, *The Annals of Albany (1850–1859)*, 7:101.

the nineteenth century, when a datestone was still readable, that the foundation for the house was laid about 1693.[3]

In 1707, Anna Barentse Staats was buried in a family cemetery on the top of the hill above the house. Joachim died in 1712. Since there was no will, the real estate went to his oldest son, Barent, who in 1701 had married Neeltje Gerritse Vandenbergh, granddaughter of the farm's previous owner. Barent and Neeltje kept a shop in Albany, but they moved to the farm after Joachim's death. A datestone on the Joachim Staats House, carrying the initials of Barent and Neeltje and the date of 1722, suggests they improved the house at that time. A visitor in 1929 found that an unreadable seventeenth-century date had been painted on the bottom of the datestone, in an apparent attempt to replace a former date that had flaked off.[4]

4. Reynolds, *Dutch Houses*, 101; New York State Library, Manuscripts and Special Collections, Staats Papers, MG 15250, Box 2, Folder 49.

Barent's will, probated in 1752, devised his property to his two surviving sons, Joachim and Gerrit, who divided the farm. Joachim, who had married Elizabeth Schuyler in 1739, took the south half, including his father's stone house. This couple probably also remodeled the house after 1752; they may have been responsible for the addition of a gambrel roof, now gone. Their initials appear on a stone at the southwest corner of the house.

Their son, Philip, inherited the house. After the Revolution, while on a tour of the country, President George Washington visited Philip Staats, one of his officers, at this house. Washington stayed for several hours while he waited for dignitaries from Albany.[5]

5. From the *Rural Repository*, reprinted in "The Minerva," vol. 3, no. 8, New Series (New-York, May 28, 1825): 113–117.

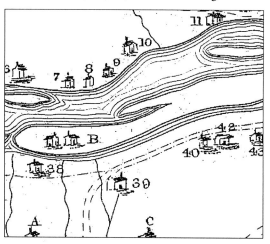

Staats descendants have continued to own and occupy the stone house and the south half of the *hooge berg* farm to the present day. The Joachim Staats House and the adjacent Gerrit Staats House are designated by letter *B* on John R. Bleeker's 1767 *Map of the Manor Renselaerwick*. The house is listed on the National Register of Historic Places.

Construction: While frame or brick country houses were the norm in both the seventeenth and eighteenth centuries on the east side of the Hudson River near Albany, the walls of the Staats House were made of coursed but irregular fieldstone of a type and quantity not available on Papscanee Island. Stone may have been brought in for the house for safety because of the French war with England that erupted locally in 1689.

In that year, residents of Papscanee had been told to prepare a fort into which they could retreat for safety in the face of French raids from Canada. Whether the fortified structure actually was built is unknown. (A fort also was ordered for Bethlehem, and others for locations in present Columbia County.) Schenectady was attacked early in 1690, and the danger continued through the decade. In 1696, the remnants of a French raiding party were captured in Schodack only a few miles away from the Staats location. Joachim Staats was active in this war.[6]

Because the Staats House was built against the shoulder of the hill, the cellar entrances are at ground level. The former location of a jambless fireplace in the east room of the main floor is indicated by a supporting arch in the ground floor below. Small bricks were used for an early rebuilding of the fireplace above the arch. The main living floor has large, double-hung windows, featuring wide, flat muntins—windows which likely date to eighteenth-century alterations. The house features mid-eighteenth-century paneling.

The roof of the house has been changed more than once. It can be assumed the structure, when occupied by the first Joachim Staats, had a steep gable roof. As fashions changed, the house was topped with a gambrel roof (probably in the mid-eighteenth century), for which framing still remains in the attic. Later, when a brick wing was added on the north side of the house, a new, shallow gable roof with a hipped west end was installed. This connected to the roof of the brick addition at the rear.

6. E. B. O'Callaghan, ed., *Documentary History of the State of New York*, 4 vols., (Albany: Weed, Parsons & Co., 1849–1851), 2:88–91.

2.2: The small porches protect entrances at ground level. The hipped end of the roof is visible at left. The square datestone appears halfway along the wide board running under the eaves.

2.3: This summer photo shows a vegetable plot and the family dog, named Tenny, on the south
side of the house.

2.4: The shallow red bricks in the east gable end, laid in Dutch cross bond, were typical of seventeenth-century construction.

2.5: The north side of the house contained a window with old shutters and a wooden eaves
   trough in the 1930s. At right is the porch of the brick wing.

THE ARIAANTJE COEYMANS HOUSE

Location: The house, on the outskirts of the present village of Coeymans in Albany County, is situated immediately north of the Coeymans Creek, close to the Hudson River.

History: Ariaantje Coeymans, born in 1672, and her brother, Samuel, born in 1670, reputedly built themselves a large house to share, probably shortly after they were allotted parts of their father's holdings in 1716 by their older brother, Andries. According to tradition, Ariaantje, a tall woman, felt liberated by her new independence, and enthusiastically carried stones for the workmen.

Ariaantje's father, Barent Pieterse (Coeymans), who established the Coeymans Patent, had died in 1710. Ariaantje and Samuel, unmarried in their late forties, may have assumed they would remain single. However, both married within a few years. As a result, they took steps to separate their joint ownership by nominal transfers of land. These actions, as well as the prohibited cutting of timber for profit on family land held in common, were challenged successfully in a lawsuit against the estate by Andries' heirs in 1785.

Ariaantje reportedly was married in her house in 1723, when she was fifty-one years old. Her husband, David Ver Planck, was twenty-eight. The marriage endured for twenty years, until her death in 1743. Ariaantje's surprising marriage to a younger man has caused so much interest that it has been overlooked that Samuel also chose a young partner, Katrina Van Schaick—twenty years his junior. Neither couple had children.

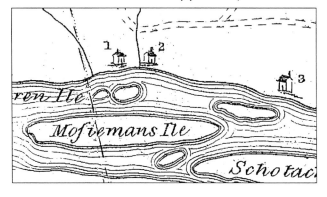

David Ver Planck and his two later wives made some use of the house after Ariaantje's death. Although Samuel had died in 1754 and David Ver Planck died in 1763, Ver Planck and Samuel Coeymans were still listed as owners of the house on the Bleeker map of 1767 (Number 2, west side).

Samuel's wife, Katrina, born in 1690, lived until 1771. The house passed to Andries Ten Eyck, a kinsman, in 1785. Andries Ten

2.6: This photo is of the back of the Ariaantje Coeymans House. The windows and rear door are
replacements or additions dating from the nineteenth century. The gambrel roof has a scuttle (opening for roof access) located near the ridge. The building at right is a
late-nineteenth-century ice house located on the Hudson River.

2.7: A detail from an eighteenth-century landscape depicting the Coeymans mills shows the east front of the Ariaantje Coeymans House (*left*). The house has Dutch-style windows and a steep roof with parapet gable ends. Steps rise to a porch by the main entrance; a door opens into the north end of the cellar (lower right corner), which served as a living or work area.

2.8: The sketch at right shows the east front of the Coeymans House as it appeared before restoration. The view is comparable to the one in the painting. Polgreen did not photograph the front of the house. Drawing by Mark Peckham, 1972.

Eyck's son, Barent, retained the house until 1864, when it was sold to Alexander E. Willis. After a succession of owners, the structure became a deteriorating tenement. However, late-twentieth-century owners have rescued and restored the historic building. Fortunately, one of these owners documented the condition of the house and identified the changes made to it.[7] The house is listed on the National Register of Historic Places.

Construction: The Coeymans House faces the Hudson River. It was built above flood level on a slope, north of the Coeymans Creek, which powered the family mill. The spacious house, fifty-six by twenty-eight feet (outside dimensions) is built of uncoursed fieldstone.

Within a few decades of its erection, the early appearance of the east front of the structure was recorded in a landscape oil painting, now lost, which also showed four mills on the creek. The artist may have been John Heaton, whose portrait of Abraham Wendell of Albany featured Wendell's mill in the back-

7. Robin Michel, "An Architectural History of the Coeymans House in Coeymans, New York, a Thesis Submitted to the Faculty of the State University of New York, College at Oneonta at its Cooperstown Graduate Programs, in partial fulfillment of requirements for the degree of Master of Arts," 1974, unpublished.

ground. Heaton probably also did the well-known Van Bergen overmantel landscape.[8]

The Ariaantje Coeymans House was depicted with a steep roof containing a large brick dormer in which were a loft door and openings for light and ventilation. Evidence for this loft door remains in the present attic. The stone walls were topped with bricks in the gable ends; parapet gable-end walls edged the roof. The roof later was changed, and the casement windows replaced. The gambrel roof shown in the photos resulted from a remodeling dating to the 1790s.

The painting of Ariaantje and Samuel Coeymans' house north of the creek showed Dutch-style casement windows, with shutters. The window openings on the first floor were examples of *kruiskozijn*. One of these early four-part windows survives, hidden in a closet inside the north gable end of the house. At present, no glass remains in either half of the window; the lower section is still covered by exterior shutters.

8. Amasa Parker, ed., *Landmarks of Albany County*, (Syracuse: D. Mason, 1897), 476. For information on Heaton's identification by Mary Black, see Blackburn, *Remembrance of Patria*, 224, 238–239, 246.

Many eighteenth-century casement windows in the Hudson Valley were like the *bolkozijn* windows shown on the second floor in the Coeymans House painting—two side-by-side rectangular openings, separated by a mullion. They appear to be not as tall as the windows on the lower floor. One side of the second-floor windows may have contained a small-paned sash that swung into the house (for light), while the other side had a shutter that opened outward (for ventilation). No second-floor casement window survives in the house today. (See the casement window of the Van Wie House, page 55, for comparison.)

Except for its extra height, Ariaantje's and Samuel's stone house was not unlike the house of their father, Barent Pieterse. His house, nicknamed the Coeymans Castle, was long (approximately fifty feet by thirty feet), built of stone, and had a similar brick roof dormer, as well as bricks in the gables. The Coeymans Castle, which stood until about 1833, was located south of the Coeymans Creek.[9]

9. Edward D. Giddings, *Coeymans and the Past* (Tri-Centennial Committee, Town of Coeymans, 1973), 33, cover, and frontispiece. See also Reynolds, *Dutch Houses*, 72; and *Landmarks of Albany County*, 476.

Because of its height, the Ariaantje Coeymans House differs from other Dutch houses in the upper Hudson Valley. It had two matching living floors, one above the other, with a garret above them. The ends of the two living floors each had a jambless fireplace. The resulting stacking of one jambless fireplace over another was more typical of the Netherlands than the Hudson Valley. Most seventeenth-century and early-eighteenth-century upper Hudson Valley Dutch houses were limited to one living story, with a garret above. Fireplaces for warmth and cooking were located in the first-floor living quarters. Because the chimney of a jambless fireplace began above it, installing another fireplace above or below presented special problems: The brick wall against which the upper fire burned had to be moved inward, to provide space for a flue from below, or an extra flue had to be carried up the outside of the house.

A frame wing now connected to the north end of the house replaced an earlier shed or barn next to the house, indicated in the oil painting. The frame wing is a very old, wooden Dutch-style house, moved to the spot, shortened to fit over a cellar, and connected to the stone house by means of a roof covering the intervening space. This roof was attached to the stone house directly across an original shuttered first-floor *kruiskozijn* window on the north wall. The roof thus preserved the window frame and shutters until the present.

2.9: The south gable end of the Coeymans House shows the broad gambrel roof that replaced an earlier roof. The brick end gable, laid in common bond, dates to the roof remodeling. Wall anchors tie the stone walls to interior framing members, indicating the floor levels.

A jambless fireplace, inserted after the frame wing was moved, suggests the wing was added before the mid-eighteenth century. The frame house, in its original (unknown) location, had a jambless fireplace, casement window frames, wall filling, and braces with curved soffits supporting exposed first-floor beams—all typical of seventeenth- and early-eighteenth-century Dutch-style frame construction in the Hudson Valley.

In 1933, the stone part of the Coeymans House was measured by the Historic American Building Survey (HABS).

2.10: This view, taken from the southwest, shows the elevated location of the Coeymans House, with ground sloping away toward both the Hudson River and the mill stream at right. The roof and chimney of the frame wing on the north end of the stone house are at left.

3.1: The front view of the Hendrick Bries House shows a porch with Victorian trim, behind which is the off-center front door. The parapet walls of the gable ends are visible, and the roof is shingled.

DUTCH-STYLE HOUSES WITH PARAPET GABLE-END WALLS

THE HENDRICK BRIES HOUSE

Location: The Hendrick Bries (*also* Bris, Breese) House is now gone. It stood until about 1939 on the east side of present Route 9J, north of Hayes Road, in East Greenbush, Rensselaer County.

History: Wyntie Van Vechten, the daughter of Johannes Van Vechten, married Hendrick Bries in 1726. Johannes portioned out his lands in 1738 among his three daughters and their husbands; however, he may have given Wyntie and her husband a house site at the time of her marriage. Johannes had inherited the south half of the farm of his father, Gerrit Teunis Van Vechten. The land was originally leased by Teunis Dirckse Van Vechten (the father of Gerrit Teunis), though the farm had been occupied by Claes Van Petten from 1680 to 1699.

A new brick house, about twenty-two and one-half feet square, with a pan-tile roof, was to be built on the farm for Claes Van Petten in 1682. In 1699, Gerrit Teunis Van Vechten leased back his father's old farm and returned to live there, probably in the house built for Van Petten. Gerrit Teunis Van Vechten's house was a well-known location on the road along the river in the early-eighteenth century, even after he died in 1704.

The house of Wyntie and Hendrick Bries does not fit the description of the 1682 house built for Claes Van Petten, lending support to the tradition that she and her husband built a new house for themselves, whether in 1726 (as tradition says) or about 1738. The two houses on the Van Vechten farm probably were close together.

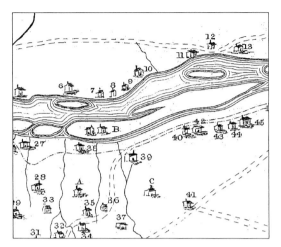

Wyntie's father, Johannes, was buried "at Papsknee" (Papscanee) in 1742. Hendrick Bries died in 1753 and also was buried in the nearby cemetery at Papsknee, thought to have been on Papscanee Island, where the Van Vechtens owned land. By the time the house of the widow Bries appeared on the 1767 Bleeker map (Number 40), the older house built for Claes Van Petten was gone. Wyntie was succeeded in ownership of her house by her son, Anthony Bries, and he by his son, John. The property, with an adjacent small island in the Papscanee Creek, was sold in 1836 by the Bries heirs to Matthew Van Benschoten Schryver.[1]

1. Rensselaer County *Deeds*, Book 41, 195–198.

Construction: The Bries House was situated parallel to the local road and to the Hudson River. It featured the parapet gable-end walls and steep roof characteristic of the Dutch-style brick houses of the period. Typically, the front door of the Bries House was slightly off-center. The house was of ample size for the period and was considerably larger than the previous house on the farm.

Although the house appeared to be made solely of brick, in fact it had a complete timber frame against which the bricks were laid. A house with this construction had the rich look and fire resistance of a brick house. The exterior bricks were laid in Dutch cross bond.

Identified as the Jan (John) Breese House (Jan Breese was the owner about 1800, but not the original owner), the house was measured by the Historic American Buildings Survey (HABS). The first-floor plan, as it existed in 1934, included two rooms—one larger than the other—and an eight-foot-wide hall with walls of brick (probably brick infill), according to the drawings. Whether these were original walls is not certain.

The stair, however, appeared to be in its original location, judging by the framing shown in the HABS plan. In the back corner of the hall, the stair, with a small landing halfway up, led to the garret. The cellar and upper garret loft level were reached by typical steep open steps. Trimmers (framing) for a smoke hood in the ceiling of the south room and the placement of the first bent (unit of framing) slightly closer to its adjacent bent than to the other

3.2: A closeup of the front window to the right of the porch shows the once-stylish *fleur de lis* wall anchors, and a shutter hook. The wall anchors are attached to the timber frame inside the bricks. Considerable repair in the bricks above both front windows indicates that earlier windows have been replaced.

bents indicated a jambless fireplace originally existed on that end of the house. The trimmers on the north end (shown in the HABS plans) suggest a jambless fireplace also existed on that end of the house. The exposed pine ceiling beams of the parlor on the south end were supported by solid braces with curved soffits, a hallmark of Dutch framing before the mid-eighteenth century.

On the rear wall of the house (according to HABS photographs and drawings not shown here), the timber frame was exposed, suggesting that the back of the house not visible from the road was originally covered by wood siding or by a frame addition.

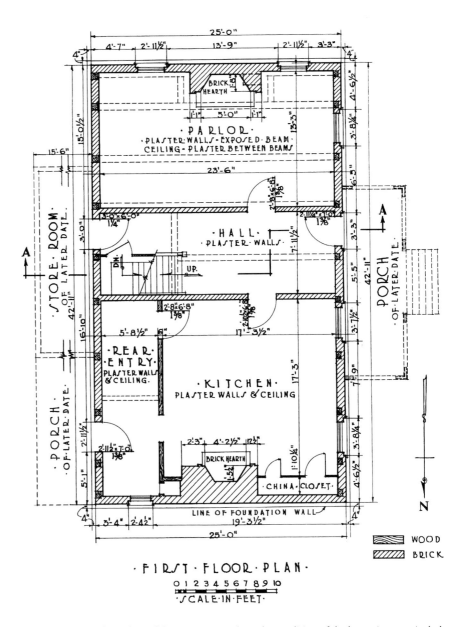

·FIRST·FLOOR·PLAN·

0 1 2 3 4 5 6 7 8 9 10
·SCALE·IN·FEET·

3.3: The HABS floor plans of the Bries House show the condition of the house in 1934, including alterations that had been made to the original, early-eighteenth-century plan. This detail shows the first floor. Note that a ceiling has been installed over the kitchen, and a rear entry added. A cross-section of the house (Section AA) is illustrated on page 18.

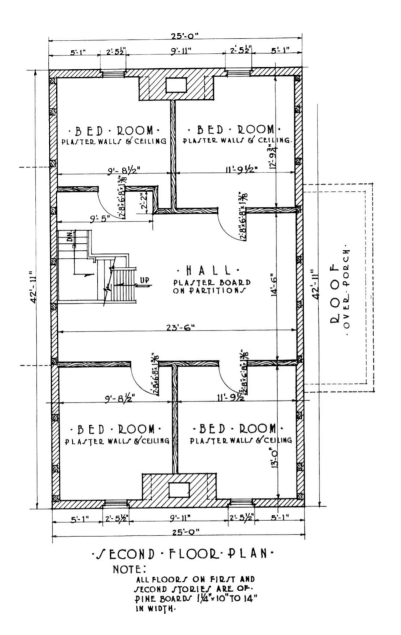

25'-0"

5'-1" · 2'-5½" · 9'-11" · 2'-5½" · 5'-1"

· B E D · R O O M ·
PLASTER WALLS & CEILING

· B E D · R O O M ·
PLASTER WALLS & CEILING.

9'-8½" 11'-9½"

12'-9¾"

2'-8×6-8×1⅜

2'-2"

9'-5"

2'-8×6-8×1⅜

42'-11"

DN.

· H A L L ·
PLASTER BOARD
ON PARTITIONS

UP

14'-6"

ROOF
· OVER · PORCH ·

42'-11"

23'-6"

2'-8×6-8×1⅜

2'-8×6-8×1⅜

9'-8½" 11'-9½"

· B E D · R O O M ·
PLASTER WALLS & CEILING

· B E D · R O O M ·
PLASTER WALLS & CEILING

13'-0"

5'-1" · 2'-5½" · 9'-11" · 2'-5½" · 5'-1"

25'-0"

· S E C O N D · F L O O R · P L A N ·

NOTE:
ALL FLOORS ON FIRST AND
SECOND STORIES ARE OF·
PINE BOARDS 1¼"×10" TO 14"
IN WIDTH·

3.4: Dotted lines on the HABS plans of the second floor indicate the tapered chimney stacks characteristic of jambless fireplaces. Wooden partitions divide the garret into bedrooms. The posts of the timber frame are shown in the outer wall of bricks.

THE HENDRICK VAN WIE HOUSE

Location: The Hendrick Van Wie House was situated south of Van Wie's Point, in Bethlehem, Albany County. Nearby on the Hudson River was *Paerde Hoeck*, now spelled Parda Hook ("Horse's Point"). The name was a result of a 1643 incident when horses fell through the ice and drowned near the point as guests made their way across the ice to a wedding party.[2] The land on which the house stood is presently owned by the federal government's Glenmont Job Corps Center.

2. A.J.F. van Laer, trans. and ed., *Minutes of the Court of Rensselaerswyck 1648–1652* (Albany: University of the State of New York, 1922), 67, 68, 203.

History: Hendrick Van Wie, born in 1703, builder of the house, was married to Catherine Waldron in October 1732. They raised ten children. The Polgreen photographs show two datestones on the east wall of the house, one of which includes the date *1732* (chalked to be visible in the photos).

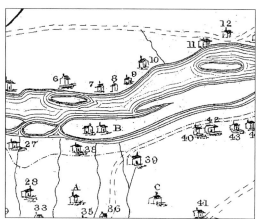

Van Wie's grandfather had settled in the area in 1675. The Bleeker map of 1767 identifies three Van Wie houses close together on the west side of the Hudson, numbered 6, 7, and 8. Hendrick Van Wie, called "Big Hendrick," lived at number 6, the southernmost residence, which seems to be this house. The house remained in the Van Wie family through the nineteenth century. Owners in the twentieth century included the Simmons family and the Knickerbocker Ice Company. Waldron Polgreen had ancestors in the Van Wie family, and was particularly interested in this house.

Construction: Polgreen's photos of the Van Wie House provide a unique record of this important Dutch residence. The pictures are particularly significant since the building was not recorded by the Historic American Buildings Survey.

The brick house was quite elegant in detail and in the 1930s retained early features, such as the decorative brick dormers and the frames for casement windows. These elements rarely survive the remodelings common to old houses. The *fleur de lis* wall anchors in the gables, however, already had been removed.[3]

3. Reynolds, *Dutch Houses*, 124.

3.5: The south wall of the brick Van Wie House is shown. The frames for large windows in the cellar and on the first floor were inserted in the nineteenth century (judging from what seem to be brownstone lintels). The four small frames with visible pegged construction above, which hold doors for lighting and ventilating the two levels of storage in the garret, probably are original. The stone section, left, is below first-floor level.

3.6: On the east front of the house, the Dutch cross bond is visible behind temporary wood scaffolding. Tarpaper wraps the roof and parapet walls on each end. Period construction details that survive include the brick dormers, a transom with four panes over the door, the tall vertical courses of brick forming lintels over the window openings and the front door, and a *bolkozijn* window frame. Two datestones are near the tops of the windows.

3.7: *(Left)* An enlarged detail of the photograph of the front of the house shows the *vlechtingen* (brick tumbling) and pinnacles of one of the brick dormers; the dormer window shown is not original. The frame has a cut-out and pintel holes for a shutter to cover the left half of the opening, and undoubtedly there was a hinged casement window opening into the house on the right. (For comparison, see the dormer windows on the Leendert Bronck House, page 66.) Polgreen chalked the datestone for visibility.

3.8: *(Right)* A detail of the first-floor Dutch-style window opening shows the wooden frame with a center mullion. Holes for the pintels that held shutters are visible. The casement windows contain glass panes held by wooden muntins. The original 1732 windows probably had smaller glass panes, set in lead.

3.9: This view of the northeast corner shows a connection to a brick addition, at right. Wall anchors (indicating the presence of a timber frame in the bricks) are visible here and in other locations.

3.10: The north wall includes ventilating holes for the upper loft level. Below them on the right side is a loft door, located as low as possible for easy access to the garret. (The door shown is not original, but the pegged frame around it is old.) There is no crane over the door, presumably since access from the ground was easy. The first-floor window (not original) has a stone lintel similar to the nineteenth-century windows on the south side of the house.

The house, near the Hudson River, was built on a rise that provided safety from floods. The ground dropped away from the foundation on the sides, permitting the cellar to open at ground level. As a result, the east front entrance had to be approached by steps. The interior plan is not known, but there were at least two rooms, indicated by two chimneys. The front door is so far to one side as to suggest the house lacked a hall. Undoubtedly, the house originally was built with a jambless fireplace in each first-floor room, and had a stair to the garret. It had the usual timber frame under the brick.

The house was being stabilized (with perhaps restoration planned) at the time Polgreen took the photographs in the 1930s, but the effort did not succeed; the structure was destroyed in the 1940s.

THE GERRIT VANDENBERGH HOUSE

Location: The Gerrit Vandenbergh House, now gone, was situated on the east side of present Route 144, south of the City of Albany, and north of the Niagara Mohawk Albany Steam Electric Plant, in Albany County. The house was north of a point on the river called *Domine's Hoeck* (Domine's Hook), an old name meaning "Parson's Point."

History: The 1767 Bleeker *Map of the Manor Renselaerwick* placed Gerrit Vandenbergh at this location (No. 11, west side). His ancestors were among

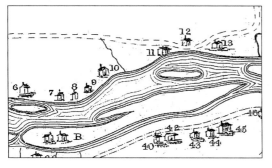

the first farmers of New Netherland. As early as 1640, Gysbert Cornelise (Vandenbergh) lived on the east side of the Hudson River in Schodack, on a farm on a hill east of present Route 9J. He subsequently farmed in Schodack on the south end of Papscanee Island. In the 1670s and 1680s, his son, Gerrit Gysbertse Vandenbergh, was the farmer on land belonging to Richard Van Rensselaer on the west side of the Hudson at Bethlehem.

By 1689, Gerrit Gysbertse was back on the east side of the river. However, in 1696 he received a perpetual lease from Kiliaen Van Rensselaer for the

3.11: This view shows the south wall of the Gerrit Vandenbergh House and its setting. The view is so similar to the photograph of this house in Reynolds' *Dutch houses in the Hudson Valley Before 1776* (page 161) that it suggests Polgreen may have tried to replicate that picture. In the pre-1929 Reynolds picture, curtains at the windows, a garden, and a well-tended landscape indicated the house was still a comfortable home. In Polgreen's 1933 photograph, the shutters and twelve-over-twelve windows are gone, and the porch has fallen down. Wall anchors have been pulled from the walls.

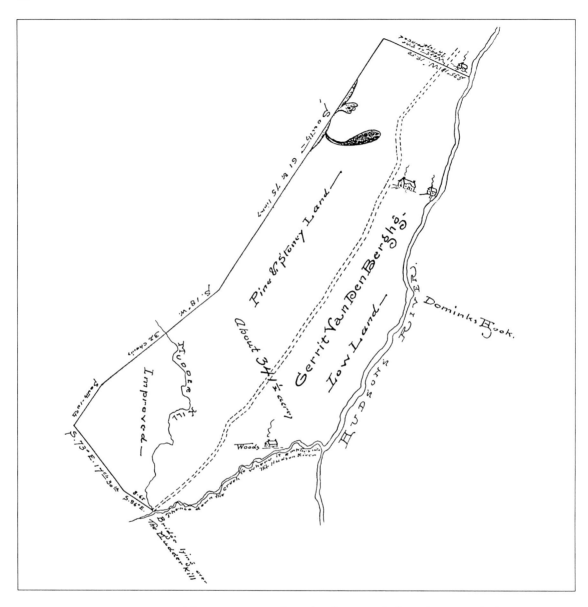

3.12: A farm survey, c.1790, shows three houses on the farm of Gerrit Vandenbergh. Of the two houses indicated by house symbols at right, the Gerrit Vandenbergh House is the one closer to the road (dotted line). Note the Mudderkill (Mud Creek), identified in the original deed of 1696. Albany County Hall of Records, *Book 17, Farm Maps and Surveys,* page 91.

Domine's Hook farm. The farm was described as "on the West side of Hudsons River to ye south of ye farm Belonging to Marte Gerretse van Bergen Deceased from thence Southwards along hudsons [*sic*] River to a Creek commonly called ye Moddrkill Running westwarde up into ye woods to ye hill Just behind said land and along said hill northward up to ye bounds of Marte Gerretse van Bergen aforesaid."[4] This description exactly fits the Gerrit Vandenbergh boundaries at Domine's Hook shown in a survey book almost one hundred years later.

On a 1697 list of the heads of households in and near Albany, no Vandenberghs were named in the Domine's Hook area. However, the family lived nearby, across the river.[5]

Gerrit Gysbertse Vandenbergh had two sons, one of whom, Gerrit Gerritse, born in 1688, married Egbertje Harmens before 1712. Apparently, it was Gerrit Gerritse who settled on the Domine's Hook farm. Gerrit Vandenbergh was in the vicinity by 1720, according to a list of freeholders, and, according to a census, a man of the same name was there in 1742.[6] In 1765, Gerrit Gerritse Vandenbergh, at age 77, gave testimony in a case involving Joachim Staats, of Papscanee Island, his brother-in-law.[7] In 1767, "Gerrit Van den Berg and son" were taxed twenty pounds—an above-average amount—for their farm and possessions.

Gerrit's son, also named Gerrit Gerritse Vandenbergh, born in 1725, married Agnietje (Annetye) Lieversen about 1747. It can be speculated that Gerrit Gerritse and Agnietje Vandenbergh built this house on the Domine's Hook farm in the 1750s. "Gerret Van de Berg and Annetye Lieversen" were original members of the congregation in 1795 when the Bethlehem Reformed Church was established.[8]

In 1796, Gerrit Vandenbergh sold the farm to Thomas Spencer. Philip Wendell bought the property in 1800; the house was owned by Wendell descendants for over one hundred years.

A barn belonging to the farm stood on the west side of present Route 144 in the twentieth century. The house was rented for almost thirty years prior to 1930 by the family of William Glaser. A member of the family recalls they lived in the frame part of the house, but used the south bedroom of the brick house. Between the wooden addition and the brick part was an old Dutch door.

A few days after the Glaser family moved away, to their dismay the old door

4. Dunn, "Settlement Patterns in Rensselaerswijck: Tracing the *Hooge Berg*," in *de Halve Maen* (spring 1995): 17; New York State Library, Manuscripts and Special Collections, Van Rensselaer Papers, "Kiliaen Van Rensselaer to Gerret Gysbertsen," Item 6982–6985.

5. Munsell, *The Annals of Albany* (1858), 9:86.

6. Munsell, *The Annals of Albany* (1870), 2:283; O'Callaghan, *Documentary History of the State of New York*, 1:246.

7. New York State Library, Manuscripts and Special Collections, Staats Papers, MG 15250, Box 2, Folder 2.

8. Florence Christoph and Peter R. Christoph, eds., *Records of the People of Bethlehem*, (Town of Bethlehem Historical Association, 1982), 108.

and the staircase from the brick house were carried off. Polgreen visited the house in 1933; his photos show the extent of ongoing vandalism. The ruins of the house were removed about 1950 by Niagara Mohawk, which developed the land for a power plant.

Construction: In profile, the Vandenbergh House looks very much like the Van Wie House. Although it does not have parapets on the gable ends, the Vandenbergh House is considered here because of this resemblance. Both houses overlooked the river, and both were situated on a rise. They were only two miles apart. Both were built into a slope, which provided easy access to a garret door on the north wall. Moreover, members of the two families had intermarried.

While the two houses had many similarities, the Vandenbergh House seems to have been built later. Architecturally, it was a transitional house. Evidence of the transitional construction included the use of both common bond and Dutch cross bond. (Polgreen wrote on the envelope that contained prints of this house, "Only part of the north gable wall and part of the adjacent west wall seem to be of the original early construction." Possibly he was referring to the confusing brick bond combination.) Three walls of the Vandenbergh House were laid in Dutch cross bond, but the south wall was done in common bond, with five rows of stretchers between each row of headers.

In the latter half of the eighteenth century, common bond, when used in conjunction with a more expensive bond, was usually relegated to parts of the house not visible from the road. The Vandenbergh House was situated very close to a well-traveled eighteenth-century public road to the northwest. This location may explain the choice of common bond for the less-visible south wall. (See the c.1753 gambrel-roofed Van Rensselaer-Genet House, page 77, for another example of this use of common bond.)

Another transitional element was the absence of brick tumbling along the slope of the roof, suggesting the roof never had parapet walls on the gable ends. In addition, the window openings were made for double-hung sash, not casement windows. Moreover, brick lintels over the windows and door were not as tall as on earlier houses, such as the Van Wie House.

However, in the old style, the Vandenbergh House had a garret door in the north gable—similar in location to a loft door in the Van Wie House and to

3.13: The south gable is laid in common bond rather than in the Dutch cross bond of the other three walls. Lintel courses of brick indicate the window openings for double-hung sash are in original locations. The tapered corners of the cellar walls are reinforced to prevent shifting. A frame wing and nineteenth-century frame additions are at the rear.

3.14: The east front carries mortises and framing for a porch. A wooden eaves trough on iron hangers has been added under the roof. Brick lintels top the window and door openings; windows at the left apparently were lengthened at a later date to open to the porch, and Greek Revival-style trim was added around the door. The timber frame under the bricks is visible at the broken sill section.

3.15: The Dutch cross bond pattern is visible on the north gable wall (*left*), now missing its garret door. As on the Van Wie House, there is no crane over this door. Apparently, outside
access was by a ladder. The Hudson River, beyond the trees, is not far away. An old roof
made of chamfered boards is under the shingles. Close examination at the roof edge
reveals beam anchors that connected the bricks to the frame. The chimney above the roof
ridge on the north end has tumbled down.

3.16: Two front entrances of the Leendert Bronck House, each topped with a four-paned transom, open on separate porches, now connected by a bridge. Brickwork alterations indicate
the first-floor windows shown are not original. Each brick dormer in the roof contains a
casement window paired with a shutter, hung with Dutch hinges. The slate roof (not original) has since been replaced with wood shingles.

one in the Gerrit Staats House. Moreover, the east facade of the Vandenbergh House retained the familiar Dutch-style off-center front entrance, above a typically high foundation, which necessitated steps to the front porch and door. According to a twentieth-century visitor, the house had two rooms on the first floor, with a hall between.[9]

9. Reynolds, *Dutch Houses*, 108.

A bedroom was located on the southerly end of the second floor, while the windowless opposite end of the second floor was used for garret storage. This second-floor layout was similar to room arrangements found in some area gambrel-roofed houses, such as the Coeymans-Bronck House.

The photographs show an old wooden roof on both the front and back of the gable. The roof covering, front and back, was made of chamfered, overlapping boards or planks, over which shingles had been laid. Some visual evidence suggests the roof had been changed. Whether this "plank roof" was the original roof, or whether another form was the original roof shape, is not certain.

THE LEENDERT BRONCK HOUSE

Location: The Leendert Bronck House is part of the Bronck Museum maintained by the Greene County Historical Society in Coxsackie, Greene County. It is south of the village of Coxsackie, on the west side of Route 9W.

History: The land at Coxsackie was obtained from the local Mohican Indians by Pieter Bronck, who built a stone house about 1663. Although he was Swedish, he had married Hilletje Jans in the Netherlands, and the family absorbed the Dutch customs of Albany, where Pieter ran a tavern and brewery. After he died in 1669, Hilletje continued to manage and lease out the farm. A son, Jan, inherited the house and farm about 1685.

Leendert Bronck, Jan's son, built this brick house in 1738 adjacent to the older stone house. The two houses were connected by an enclosed passageway. Leendert and his wife, Anna de Wandelaer, married in 1717, had five children. Their oldest son, Jan Leendert, was born in 1723. Jan Leendert, who married Elsie Van Buren, was the next son to inherit the house, along with part of the land. His portion of the farm remained in the Bronck (sometimes spelled Bronk) family into the twentieth century. A descendant, Leonard Bronk Lampman, donated the houses, barns and acreage to the Greene County Historical Society in 1939. The houses do not appear on the Bleeker map of 1767 because they were south of Rensselaerswyck.

No photographs of the 1663 stone house were included with Polgreen's negatives, although he took several pictures of the brick house and one of the porch on the addition to the stone house. Polgreen included a picture of Jessie Van Vechten Vedder seated on this south porch. She had led a fight to save the stone bridge at Leeds, and had been Town of Catskill Historian, Catskill Village Historian, and Greene County Historian. She wrote a county history and helped organize the Greene County Historical Society, the fledgling organization that took possession of the Bronck Houses in 1939.[10]

The Bronck Museum, including houses, outbuildings, and a Dutch barn, is a National Historic Landmark.

Construction: The gable ends of the Leendert Bronck House have the European profile of early-eighteenth-century Dutch-style houses near Albany. The house had jambless fireplaces located back-to-back in the center of the building, rather than at each end. (For another example of this type of chimney location, see the Teunis Slingerland House, page 73.)

The house featured two front doors, divided horizontally in the Dutch style, one opening into each large first-floor room, with no center hall. An interior door now connects the two first-floor rooms.

The house is constructed of bricks laid around a timber frame. The large pine ceiling beams in the first-floor rooms, mortised into the wall posts, are supported at each end by typical solid corbels with curved soffits. Two corbels, however, were left off when the house was built. The stair to the garret, once enclosed, is located in the southeast corner of the south room.

10. *The Quarterly Journal*, Greene County Historical Society, Coxsackie, N.Y., 7:3 (fall, 1983): 22; and 7:4 (winter, 1983): 38. Additional information is from conversations with Shelby Kriele, curator of the Bronck Museum.

3.17: A Dutch-style porch, with a cantilevered roof, is located on an addition attached to the Pieter Bronck House. The seated woman is Jessie Van Vechten Vedder, Greene County Historian, who was instrumental in establishing the Bronck Museum and the Greene County Historical Society.

3.18: Polgreen's view of the southeast corner of the house shows the classic Dutch "spoutgable" typical of the 1730s. The stone coping or cover on the top surface of the gable wall has been added to keep out moisture. Wall anchors indicate the timber framing.

3.19: Each of the parapet gable-end walls is topped with a brick pinnacle which does not contain a chimney, since that is in the center. *Vlechtingen* line the angle of the parapet wall, which ends in a "knee," a horizontal section. A shutter of a type dating to the eighteenth century hangs on the window in the passageway connecting the brick house to the older stone house at left.

THE TEUNIS SLINGERLAND HOUSE

Location: The house is situated near the Onesquethaw Creek, two miles south-west of Feura Bush, on the southeast side of Route 32, in Albany County.

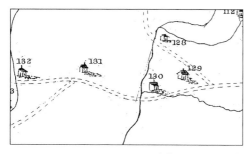

History: In 1762, the house was owned by Teunis Slingerland, according to a datestone. The 1767 Bleeker map also placed him at this location (No. 130, west side). Teunis was a grandson of Teunis Cornelis Slingerland, who, with Johannes Appel, bought a large tract on the Onesquethaw Creek from the Indians in 1685. In 1687, Teunis Cornelis was residing outside of Albany on the Normanskill when he gave his two younger sons portions of the Onesquethaw tract. According to the document, building was going on at Onesquethaw; finishing a barn was mentioned.[11]

In 1701, however, Teunis Cornelis was living at Hackensack when he transferred his remaining rights to the land at Onesquethaw to Cornelis Slingerland, his oldest son. Cornelis was described in the deed as a blacksmith residing in Schenectady.[12] Married to Eva Mebie (Mabee) of Schenectady in 1699, Cornelis was in the Onesquethaw area by 1742, according to a list of freeholders. He died at Onesquethaw in 1753.

The son of Cornelis and Eva, named Teunis, born in 1723, was the owner of the house under discussion. He married Agnietje Witbeck by 1747, and died in 1800. The brick and stone house of Teunis and Agnietje remained in the Slingerland family through the nineteenth century, and is now occupied by descendants. It is listed on the National Register of Historic Places.

Construction: The house is of coursed stone on the sides, with brick gable ends laid in Dutch cross bond. Back-to-back jambless fireplaces were located in the center of the house, between front and back rooms. There was no hall.

Although located in the country, with its front entrance in the south gable end, the house had the orientation and room layout of an urban structure built on a narrow city lot. The house faced an old road, now gone, which ran from the Helderberg hills to the Hudson River. Consequently, only its side and rear walls are visible from the modern road.

11. *Dutch Settlers Society of Albany Yearbook*, 13 (1937–1938): 11. See also Peter R. Christoph, *A Norwegian Family in Colonial America* (Higginson Book Co., 1994), 139.

12. New York State Library, Manuscripts and Special Collections, Papers of A.J.F. Van Laer, MP 15317, Box 8.

3.21: Brick arches over windows were common in early brick houses, but, in this case, arches
were not used in the brick gable ends, but rather on the stone section. The window on the
right retains its casement form; the window on the left has been altered. Note the center
chimney.

Architectural evidence indicates the roof formerly had a parapet wall on the south gable end; when the roof was remodeled, the parapet was removed or covered. Wall anchors appear on the stone sides and the gable ends. The loft openings and windows are topped with tall lintel courses of vertical bricks, and both loft openings and first-floor window frames, with a center mullion, accommodated casement windows or shutters. The window openings are similar to those of the 1732 Van Wie House. A transom with five glass panes is set into the frame over the front door.

The construction details enumerated above suggest a date of erection for the Teunis Slingerland House earlier than the date of 1762 on the rear wall would indicate. Except for its gable-to-road orientation and its unusual brick-and-stone combination, the house mimics area Dutch-style farmhouses built prior to 1750. An enclosed corner staircase leading from the front room to the garret is retained in the Slingerland House. The stair paneling is similar to that found in the gambrel-roofed houses of the 1750s and 1760s. The paneling, if original, would support the 1762 date; more likely, the paneling could have been part of an update at that time if the house had been built earlier.

3.22: The southeast gable wall is the original front. Hidden in the shrubbery is a cellar door, above which the front entrance requires steps. The framed roof with heavy moldings, overhang, and roof returns dates to the nineteenth century, but the tips of *vlechtingen* from eighteenth-century construction are visible. The base of a brick finial, on which commonly was mounted a crane for lifting objects to the garret, survives at the peak under the later roof of the Teunis Slingerland House. A similar brick finial appeared on the Lansing House, also known as Pemberton's Store, built in Albany in 1710.[13] Both the finial and *vlechtingen* indicate that the south gable of the house formerly had a parapet gable wall.

13. Reynolds, *Dutch Houses*, 117; Blackburn, *Remembrance of Patria*, 113.

4.1: Waldron Polgreen climbed the ridge behind the Van Rensselaer-Genet House to capture views of the wide meadows beyond. Papscanee Island lies to the west, indicated by the low knoll in the distance at left. Beyond, barely visible, is the Hudson River. The ribbon-like stream crossing the field was called the Mill Brook; a mere trickle today, in the seventeenth century it ran a mill and required a bridge to carry the road across it.

DUTCH-INFLUENCED GAMBREL-ROOFED HOUSES

THE VAN RENSSELAER-GENET HOUSE

Location: The Van Rensselaer-Genet House was situated on the east side of present Route 9J, north of Hayes Road, in East Greenbush, Rensselaer County. It burned about 1940.

History: The seventeenth-century farm of Teunis Dirckse Van Vechten, extending north of present Hayes Road, was established in 1639. It was divided between grandsons Johannes and Volckert Van Vechten after the death of their father, Gerrit Teunis Van Vechten, in 1704. The south half of the farm went to Johannes; in 1749, Kiliaen H. Van Rensselaer, son of Hendrick Van Rensselaer of Crailo (in the present city of Rensselaer), bought from the heirs of Johannes Van Vechten a large part of the farm which had been Johannes' inheritance. (The land was not part of the Rensselaerswyck grant that Kiliaen's father received in 1704.)

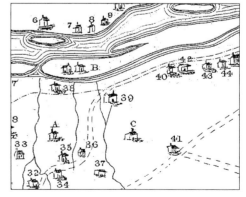

In 1742, Kiliaen H. Van Rensselaer had married Ariaantje Schuyler. Her sister, the wife of Joachim Barentse Staats, lived on the south end of Papscanee Island, not far from the site where Kiliaen and Ariaantje built this brick house about 1753.

The Van Rensselaer House remained in the family for about fifty years. It is indicated on Bleeker's 1767 *Map of the Manor Renselaerwick* as No. 39, east side.

The sons of Kiliaen and Ariaantje were Hendrick K., Philip, Nicholas, and Kiliaen K. After the senior Kiliaen

1. A.J.F. Van Laer, ed., *The Van Rensselaer Bowier Manuscripts* (Albany: University of the State of New York, 1908), 741. The deeds are at the Albany Institute of History and Art, McKinney Library, FB 780 /2 /5.

4.2: The house of c. 1753, in its setting along the River Road, faced west. The ridge behind it limited the size of seventeenth-century farms in the area. The flat fields between the ridge and the river, however, were prized by early Dutch farmers. A list of Rensselaerswyck leases one hundred years earlier described this farm, then occupied by tenant Teunis Dirckse Van Vechten, as "one of the best."[1]

moved to a frame house (now gone) on the ridge to the east, the 1753 brick house was occupied by his son, Hendrick, whose wife was Alida Bradt.

Early in the nineteenth century, the brick Van Rensselaer-Genet House became the property of Edmond Charles Genet, known as Citizen Genet, a gadfly French diplomat who tried to spur American involvement in the French Revolution. Unable to return to France, Genet married Cornelia Clinton, daughter of George Clinton, New York governor and subsequent vice-president of the United States. As a local farmer, investor and scientific innovator, Genet planned a canal to improve shipping near Greenbush; this canal would have improved navigation along the stretch of the Hudson adjacent to his own land, but it was never dug.

With the Van Rensselaer House, Genet acquired 600 acres and he later bought more land. Genet considered the Van Rensselaer House old fashioned, and after a decade he moved to another house nearby. However, Genet's descendants retained the old brick house and the farm into the twentieth century. Polgreen visited and photographed the house in more than one season.

Construction: Tradition holds that Kiliaen H. Van Rensselaer built the house. Since he did not buy the land until 1749, it is likely he built his house after that date. Polgreen wrote on the envelope containing some prints of this house, "One brick in front wall incised 1753; another incised 17 E VR ( ) o." The 1753 date seems appropriate in light of the purchase information and the architectural style.

The gambrel-roofed house had a timber frame inside the bricks, in the Dutch manner. The bricks were laid in traditional Dutch cross bond, despite the new-style gambrel roof. Later gambrels, by widening the roof span, permitted extra depth on the first floor as well as in the garret, but this house was not exceptionally deep. The house, instead, was long in comparison with earlier Dutch-style houses. Although there were two rooms on each side of a center hall, the rooms must have been small; approximate exterior dimensions of the collapsed foundation, which remains on the site today, are twenty-three feet by forty-eight feet.

As Polgreen's thorough photographs of the house show, no bake ovens protruded through the end walls. This suggests that at least one of the first-floor fireplaces was jambless, in the manner of other early area gambrels.

4.3: Dutch cross bond is used on the front and sides. The south gable shows the steep angle of the lower section of the roof, with a narrow top, characteristic of an early gambrel in a Dutch area.

4.4: In the north gable of the house are oval ventilating holes. These are not gun ports, as is
sometimes thought. Instead, they offered ventilation and light to a section of unheated garret used for storage.

4.5: The house front and north gable are shown from the northwest. The bricks had been given a coat of paint or mastic. Although the windows shown are not original, the house was built with double-hung sash, rather than with Dutch-style casement windows.

4.6: The house has no kitchen wing or additions except the small back porch, shown here. The rear wall, not visible from the road, was laid in a utilitarian common bond, in contrast to the more expensive Dutch cross bond of the front and sides. A cellar entrance is under the window at left.

THE GERRIT STAATS HOUSE

Location: The brick shell of the house stands on the south part of Papscanee Island, on Staats Island Road, in Schodack, Rensselaer County.

History: The 1749 will of Barent Staats, son of Joachim Staats (see the Joachim Staats House, page 31) divided his farm between his two sons,

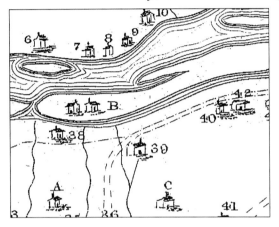

Joachim and Gerrit. The younger Joachim retained the lower half of the farm and the stone house of his father; Gerrit Staats, born in 1722, received other sections of the farm. He and his wife, Deborah Beekman, built this brick house north of the knoll called the *hooge berg* in 1758, according to a date and initials on the outside wall near the west door.[2] The Gerrit Staats and Joachim Staats Houses are indicated on Bleeker's 1767 map as Letter B on Papscanee Island.

Gerrit Staats' will, written in 1805, divided his farm between sons Barent G. and Jacob. Barent received the section with the brick house; John Schryver became the next owner of the parcel containing the house. Schryver's son, George, sold the land and house in 1853 to Peter L. Muller, of Albany.[3]

Waldron Polgreen's photographs are a valuable record of this little-known house. In the decade after the pictures were taken in the 1930s, the gambrel roof was replaced. The altered house was occupied until it burned in December 1973. The ruined shell is listed on the National Register of Historic Places as part of a National Register District, which includes the Joachim Staats House and the Staats Cemetery.

Construction: The steep pitch of the gambrel roof of the house was comparable to the roof on the Van Rensselaer-Genet House, built by relatives a mile away only a few years earlier. The Gerrit Staats House was similar in depth to the Van Rensselaer-Genet House, but ten feet shorter in length. The off-center entrance of the Staats House echoed the entrances of older brick houses in the area. In 1929, a visitor reported that on the first floor there was

2. Reynolds, *Dutch Houses*, 102.

3. Rensselaer County, *Deeds*, Book 19:292–293, Book 85:424, Book 35, 362-363.

4.7: Windows of the west front of the Gerrit Staats House, facing the Hudson River, have been replaced. The second window from the right has been closed up, while a small window has been inserted by the door. The house has been painted, or covered with mastic, which is wearing off. Over the corner of the porch, a small datestone, reportedly bearing the date of 1758, is visible.

4.8: The south gable end retains early pegged frames at both levels of the garret, holding either casement windows or shutters. A pegged frame intended for a double-hung window is on the first floor. Brick arches indicate these are original locations.

4.9: The north gable end clearly shows the Dutch cross bond; plain anchors attach the brick wall to the interior timber frame. The first-floor window on the north end, lacking the arch of the openings on the south gable, is not original. The loft door has been remodeled to make a window, but it retains part of its early pegged frame. Below the loft door is an area of brick repair. Over the front door, a transom with four panes is nearly hidden in shadow. The old dormers have center mullions, suggesting casement sash.

4. Reynolds, *Dutch Houses*, 102.

a hall, with one room to the north and two on the south.[4] Except for the "new" gambrel-style roof, construction details reprised those of the previous Dutch-style houses in the area. A low loft door on the north gable was similar in location to the loft doors on the Van Wie and Vandenbergh Houses. In addition, the Gerrit Staats House had a timber frame (which still can be seen in the ruins) under the bricks, vertical lintels of brick over the front window openings and brick arches over other windows, a transom with glass panes over the door, and exterior brick laid in Dutch cross bond.

THE TOBIAS TEN EYCK HOUSE

Location: The house stands on the east side of Old Ravena Road (Pictuay Road), halfway between Selkirk and Ravena, in Albany County, near the Coeymans Creek.

History: The house was built about 1760 by Tobias C. Ten Eyck on land he had received from his uncle, Samuel Coeymans. Samuel Coeymans and his wife, Katrina Van Schaick, had no children. Ten Eyck, born in 1723, was the son of Katrina's sister, Gerritje, and Coenradt J. Ten Eyck, the Albany silversmith. Other family ties were close; the mother of Coenradt was Geertruy Coeymans. The farm of Tobias Ten Eyck was within the original Coeymans Patent of 1673. Formerly, a road connected this house with the Coeymans property.

Tobias Ten Eyck was a gunsmith by trade, but he also owned the sloop *Criestiena* that carried produce to New York prior to 1760. In the 1750s, according to family tradition, Tobias lived across the creek in a house built earlier. The next-to-youngest of ten children, he had been "packed off to the country to settle down."[5] Some of his profits from hauling freight and war supplies on the Hudson River during the French and Indian Wars in the 1750s are thought to have been put into his new house, shown in the photographs. Tradition says that bricks for the house were made from clay dug on the farm.

Fortunately, Tobias kept a bound shipping record for the sloop, including entries in both Dutch and English. The book, passed down in the

5. S. Niles Haight, "The Eight Onesquethaw Houses," unpublished manuscript. Haight was a descendant of the Vanderzee family, and interested in genealogy.

4.10: The original window openings of the Tobias Ten Eyck House are topped with lintels of vertical bricks. The boxed lintels and doorway surround date to the mid-nineteenth-century remodeling. The windows appear to be replacements for original double-hung sash.

Coeymans and Polgreen families, became Waldron Polgreen's treasured possession. Polgreen wrote an article about this record book for the *Dutch Settlers' Society Yearbook*, noting that Ten Eyck's records "were not the careful notations of a merchant, but of a well-to-do farmer who owned a sloop on the river for his own convenience. . . . As an accommodation to his relatives, Tobias apparently ran mercantile errands and occasionally bought and sold for friends during the years 1753 through 1755. Then war in 1756 brought strange cargoes to the *Criestiena*."[6] The volume of shipping records was presented to the Greene County Historical Society's Vedder Library in 1992 by Waldron Polgreen's son, Richard.

6. *Dutch Settlers' Society of Albany Yearbook*, 20 (1944-45): 16.

In 1756, Tobias married Judickie Van Buren, from Schodack, across the river. He was killed in 1791, according to family lore, when a gun he had

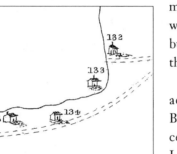

made exploded in his face while he was hunting wild turkeys in the Pictuay. He and his wife are buried in a family cemetery on a hillside south of the house; there is also a slave cemetery nearby.

Ten Eyck's property once encompassed 1,300 acres in the Pictuay area of the town of Bethlehem. The house sits beside an eighteenth-century road from Onesquethaw to Coeymans Landing; the Coeymans Creek curves north of the house. On the 1767 Bleeker map, the Tobias Ten Eyck location is indicated at No. 135, west side. The house is listed on the National Register of Historic Places.

Construction: The large, story-and-a-half, five-bay house with its gambrel roof faces west. In profile, the top of the gambrel is broader than the gambrels on the Van Rensselaer-Genet and Gerrit Staats Houses. A sizable brick extension at the rear appears to be original. The walls were laid in Dutch cross bond on all sides, including the extension.

The brick band above the windows across the front is a Georgian architectural feature. It is suggestive of a decorative brick belt course above the windows on another period gambrel, the Van Schaick House, near present Cohoes. The Van Schaicks were related to Tobias Ten Eyck through his mother. Anthony Ten Eyck, the brother of Tobias, also built a brick gambrel-roofed house in Schodack Landing, across the river. The large size and Georgian brick details of the Ten Eyck houses were costly; the Ten Eyck and Van Schaick examples of this architectural style strongly suggest family members copied each other's homes.

As evidence of the transitional architectural trends near the close of the French and Indian Wars, the south room of the first floor of the Tobias Ten Eyck House was built with a traditional jambless fireplace, indicated by the brick arch springing from the cellar wall under the hearth, while the north room, shown in the Polgreen photograph, boasted a jambed fireplace surrounded by period paneling. This north fireplace was supported in the cellar by brick piers.

4.11: The first-floor windows in the north gable and in the rear extension have no brick lintels and appear to have been added, while upstairs the openings were enlarged. The gable of the house carries the initials *T C TE*, for Tobias Coenradt Ten Eyck. Vestigial brick triangles, although no longer needed to protect the wall, were placed along the slopes of the roof.

4.12: A rear view of the house shows a window has been replaced on the south wall of the wing. Part of the rear foundation has been repaired with brick. A scuttle can be seen on the roof at center.

4.13: Molded curved bricks connect the top edge of the foundation with the brick walls. These specially designed water-table bricks appear on other area gambrel-roofed houses. The brick walls are load-bearing and lack the traditional interior timber frame.

4.14: The front door, slightly off-center, leads to a hall, with Dutch-style divided doors at the front and rear. The roof overhang and roof brackets date to a Victorian update in the mid-nineteenth century. A cellar entrance, left, has been closed up.

4.15: Polgreen took two interior photos of this house, the only interior photos in his collection. The unusual stair, with its scalloped trim and beaded boards, is at the front corner of the hall, and rises over the front door.

4.16: The north first-floor room shows the Georgian-style paneling and mantel, both of which are typical of mid-eighteenth-century construction. The molding of the mantel is hidden by the stove pipe. The fireplace opening, behind the stove, has been closed off.

4.17: A pent roof covers a doorway with double-hung side windows of the Coeymans-Bronck House. Polgreen had photographed the addition to the Pieter Bronck House, which had a similar roof and porch with seats. The Federal-style trim and tracery above the front door shown here are part of an early update, which included parts of the interior of the house. At left is a wooden addition.

THE COEYMANS-BRONCK HOUSE

Location: The house is on the south end of the village of Coeymans, on the east side of Route 144, overlooking the Hudson River.

History: The property was once part of the Coeymans Patent. Pieter B. Coeymans, son of Barent Pieterse Coeymans, received this part of his father's estate in 1716. The first known owners of the house were Charlotte Coeymans Bronck, born in 1727, daughter of Pieter B. Coeymans, and her husband, Jan Jonas Bronck. They married in 1760.

The house is believed to have been erected late in the 1760s. The present owners, in reconstructing the original door sill on the east side of the house, found a coin dated 1767 beneath the sill, giving a possible date of construction.

Charlotte Amelia was the third child of Charlotte and Jan Bronck. She married John Teunis Van Dalfsen, a soldier in the Revolutionary War and the War of 1812, and first supervisor of the town of Coeymans. They resided in this house, after which it descended through Van Dalfsen family connections until it was sold in the 1860s to the Niles family. Members of that family resided in the house for 113 years.

There was only one photo of this house in the Polgreen collection; he may have visited the house because of the Coeymans and Bronck connections in his ancestry.

Construction: The one-and-a-half-story stone house with a gambrel roof fronts the Hudson River, leaving only its rear entrance visible from the present public road. The gambrel roof is broader than the roofs of the Van Rensselaer-Genet and Gerrit Staats houses of a decade earlier. The Coeymans-Bronck House was built with double-hung sash windows; early nine-over-nine sashes survive on the west side. In a pattern that became typical in the 1760s, one bedroom, with a fireplace, is located on the south end of the second story.

With its broad center hall and decorative staircase, the house has elements of Georgian style as well as some Dutch features, such as a Dutch door with early hardware and a stoop (porch) at the riverside entrance. One first-floor room retains 1760s paneling.

5.1: Only one photograph of the Van Sante-Bleeker House was included with the Polgreen collection. The house is made of coursed fieldstone and limestone blocks. The abbreviated windows of the second floor/attic, and one of the windows beside the front door are visible. Twelve-pane windows give light to the first floor.

THE WANING DUTCH INFLUENCE

THE VAN SANTE-BLEECKER HOUSE

Location: The house, located beside the Onesquethaw Creek, is on the south side of Onesquethaw Creek Road, southwest of the village of Feura Bush, in Albany County.

History: Tradition states that this house was built as an outpost to protect the southwest area of the Manor of Rensselaerswyck during the French and Indian Wars of the 1750s; there are tales that prisoners of those wars were kept here. The unusual architecture of the house lends support to these stories, though no documentation has been found: The cellar includes small rooms with heavy doors; some windows in the basement area are barred; and the second floor/attic area is one large, barracks-type room with a fireplace and wooden pegs for hanging clothes.

The Bleeker map of 1767 shows a structure in this approximate location with the name of Hendrick Karn (No. 121, west side). Hendrick Karn (also Carel, Carr) was listed on the muster rolls of the area in 1759. A connection is noted between Karn and Gerrit Van Sante, whose brother, Gysbert, was married to Margrietje Karn, apparently Hendrick Karn's daughter. The building possibly appears on other maps—for example, although it is not identified, it is likely that it is one of a group of six buildings on

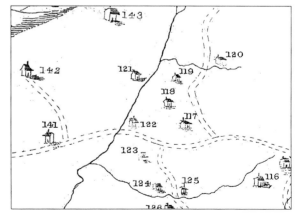

the Coeymans Creek at Niscotha (Onesquethaw) indicated on c.1757 maps prepared for the British Army.[1]

Nevertheless, when the wars were over, the stone structure became a farmhouse. In his will, dated April 4, 1806, Gerrit Van Sante devised to his grandson, Gerrit Van Sante Bleecker, "my farm at Niscadhaw [Onesquethaw], County of Albany, which I purchased from Stephen Van Rensselaer and his late father." In 1806, Stephen Van Rensselaer III, the last patroon, was the proprietor of Rensselaerswyck. Since Stephen Van Rensselaer II died in 1769, Gerrit Van Sante must have obtained the 148-acre Onesquethaw farm prior to 1769, shortly after it was occupied by Hendrick Karn. Van Sante had leased a different farm in Bethlehem in August 1769, which he later sold. A confirming lease for the Onesquethaw farm was given to Gerrit Van Sante December 27, 1785, by Stephen Van Rensselaer III.[2]

In addition to this house on his country farm, Van Sante had a home in Albany. He was a trader in Albany, and was Commissioner of Stores for the British Army in North America from 1767 to 1775. His farm, and those of his neighbors along the Onesquethaw Creek, may have produced some of the pork and flour he sold to the English army prior to the Revolutionary War.

The house is presumed to have been constructed about 1755, at the opening of hostilities with the French, before Van Sante's occupancy. The house is listed on the National Register of Historic Places.

Construction: The stone house, which gives evidence of having been built for some special purpose, should be compared to the fortified mansions along the Mohawk River built by Sir William Johnson and members of his family.

Although it is not a conventional Georgian house, its details are Georgian. Dutch influence is limited to beaded beams, a few Dutch hinges, a divided entrance door, and a frame wing in Dutch style at the rear. The main building has a high basement, a first floor divided by a broad hall, and a combined second floor and attic which make a single finished room fifty-eight feet by thirty-six feet. The attic room has an original fireplace at one end. To create this large space, the gable roof is supported by a series of trusses with king-posts and angled bracing. There is no ceiling, but the unusual trusses may have been partially floored for storage.

The basement, with an entrance at ground level, contains one jambed

1. New York State Library, Manuscripts and Special Collections, Crown Collection, c. 1757; Huntington Library, San Marino, CA, "A Map of the Province of New York and Part of New Jersey," HM 15453. References to militia and tax lists are from Florence Christoph, *Upstate New York in the 1760s* (Camden, Maine: Picton Press, 1992).

2. Albany County Hall of Records, *Wills*; Albany County Hall of Records, *Book 17, Farm Maps and Surveys*, 101.

stone fireplace. Stone partitions set off small rooms with battened doors hung with unique tapered hinges. Large beaded beams under the rooms and cross-framing under the hall support the first floor. The well-finished beams and fireplace indicate the basement was intended as a living floor.

The front entrance, framed with narrow windows, opens to a wide hall with two rooms on each side. English-style jambed fireplaces warm the larger rooms; one fireplace retains a period Georgian-style mantel from the mid-eighteenth century. From the stair landing at the rear of the hall, steps lead down to the frame building at rear, and directly up to the second floor/attic.

Attached to the rear of the stone building is a small Dutch-style frame building, with smoothly planed, beaded first-floor beams. No corbels (braces) are visible. Possibly used as a kitchen, the frame wing once had a jambless fireplace and has its own cellar.

Other structures that were part of the complex are indicated by foundations. The farm's Dutch barn, which deteriorated and was torn down in the 1970s, was replaced by the current owners in 1990 with the Larger Wemp barn, a classic Dutch barn moved from Fort Hunter, Montgomery County, New York.

THE ALBERT VANDERZEE HOUSE

Location: The house is on Rowe Road, near Feura Bush, about one mile southwest of the village, off Onesquethaw Creek Road, in Albany County.

History: The Harmen Vanderzee farm included some of the land along the Onesquethaw Creek that was part of the extensive Teunis Cornelis Slingerland-Johannes Appel purchase of 1685. The segment came from Teunis Cornelis' son, Cornelius, to Cornelius' daughter, Eve. She married Harmen Vanderzee in 1737; he was the son of Albert Storm Vanderzee, and grandson of Storm (Bradt) Vanderzee and Harmen Gansevoort of Albany. The location of Harmen Vanderzee is shown on Bleeker's 1767 map (No. 122, west side).

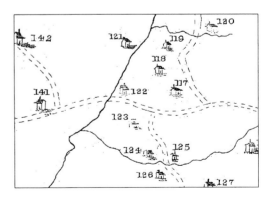

3. S. Niles Haight, "The Eight Onesquethaw Houses"; also map of eighteenth-century surveys by Christopher Albright, 1994.

Harmen Vanderzee was succeeded on his farm by his son, Albert, who, according to one unpublished family account, "is usually given credit for building the house." On a survey of the farm dated 1787, "Albert's house" is noted.[3] Albert, born in 1738, did not come into possession of the property officially until after his father's death, around 1788, when he and his brother each inherited a half interest. Albert bought out his brother's interest in the farm in 1798. Albert's son, Henry, called the house "my mansion home" in his 1838 will.

According to family tradition, the Vanderzee house descended through six generations of Vanderzees until it was sold by Harmen Vanderzee in 1953. The house is listed on the National Register of Historic Places.

Construction: The large, two-story house, which faces south, is built of rectangular stone blocks and bricks. Originally, the house was smaller and did not have a center hall. Early in the nineteenth century the house was greatly enlarged; stone blocks were used to face the front of the addition, while bricks laid in common bond were used for the addition's gable end and back.

The stone section of the house bears a datestone with the initials *AVDZ* (Albert Vanderzee) and the date of 1804. However, the original date of construction of the house is believed to be earlier. It is clear on the interior that the stone section is older than the brick addition. In the west room, a Federal-style fireplace mantel has dentil molding and matching paneling, similar to a mantel and paneling in the Moak-Leedings House in nearby Feura Bush.

A Dutch-style divided entrance door opens to the center hall of the Vanderzee House. Old window frames survive on the back of the older part of the house, and Dutch hinges appear on a door in the cellar and on shutters in the attic.

5.2: The front view shows the Albert Vanderzee House before purchase and restoration by Dr. and Mrs. George Righter. A nineteenth-century carriage house is attached at the left. Lower windows have been replaced with single-pane sash.

5.3: A rear view of the structure shows part of the brick addition (*left*) and the older stone section (*right*). Shutters are closed in the pegged window frames on the first floor. A frame kitchen wing is at left.

5.4: The west end of the Vanderzee House is shown, with wooden additions from the nineteenth
century. There are no windows in this older end of the house, although the attic has openings for light and ventilation.

5.5: Evaline Wiltsie Vanderzee posed in the front door for Polgreen; her death in 1934 dates the photograph to that year or earlier. Her son, Harmen, was the last of the Vanderzee owners. A seam in the stone to the right of the door, between the addition (*right*) and the earlier section (*left*) is barely visible.

5.6: The brick end of the house, laid in common bond, is visible from the present road. Federal-style quarter-round openings with glass panes light the attic, and stone quoins, at left, connect the stone front to the bricks. The brick end of the house was added in the nineteenth century.

5.7: A corner of the homestead's barn is shown at far right in this view from the fields.

5.8: A view of surrounding farmland from the front of the house shows the barn and the bridge that carries Rowe Road over the Onesquethaw Creek.

5.9: An unknown person is almost hidden behind a stone fence at the rear of the house. The barn is at right.

5.10: The house, outbuildings, and the Onesquethaw Creek are viewed looking north toward the house from the fields.

5.11: This view of the Moak-Herber House shows the two-family shed kitchen addition, with two entrance doors and individual chimneys. The stone section of the house, at right, contains an interesting narrow window. A well pump stands at each end of the wing.

THE MOAK-HERBER HOUSE

Location: The house, gone since 1968, was located on the southeast side of Route 32 at Feura Bush, along the present entrance road to the General Electric Plastics Division Manufacturing Plant.

History: In the last quarter of the eighteenth century, farm surveys and deed books show four large farm holdings of Moak families at the present village of Feura Bush. The village was listed as "Moakville" on the 1851 Pease map of Albany County. Jacob Moak, born in Switzerland, apparently came to America in 1732 with a brother, Frans, and other family members, including a relative named Johannes (John). They were with a shipload of Palatines who had embarked from Rotterdam, the Netherlands. Jacob's first child, Henry, was baptized at Albany in 1740. Henry Moak, Frans Moak, and John Moak were listed on the Rensselaerswyck militia rolls of 1759 among Feura Bush area neighbors. Jacob was also listed, but in another neighborhood.

On the southeast side of the Onesquethaw Road (present Route 32), Frans Moak, who had married Engeltie Slingerland, leased forty-five acres on January 28, 1788. According to an earlier survey, Frans and Engeltie already had a house (now gone) on the site by 1776, near the center of present Feura Bush.[4]

On the same side of the road as Frans Moak's house, his son, Johannes F. Moak, leased sixty-one acres on December 28, 1787, and ninety-three and two-fifths acres on July 14, 1797. The Moak-Herber house was occupied by Johannes Moak (or Johannes Mog, as he signed the 1797 lease).[5] His land later was leased to Nicholas Moak, probably a son.

The graves of Nicholas Moak, born in 1778, and his wife, Rosana Brate, born in 1780, located near the house, were removed to the Jerusalem Cemetery in Feura Bush in 1918. Family tradition states that the Moak-Herber House was built prior to the Revolution and was lived in by Moak descendants until 1891.

The railroad ran through the property in 1865, and in 1926 the New York Central railroad yards were built, taking a large section of the farm nearest the village. The old house and thirty acres were left; however, when this acreage was taken by General Electric in 1968, the frame and stone house and a large Dutch barn were demolished.

4. Albany County Hall of Records, *Book 18, Farm Maps and Surveys*, 117; see also *Book 17* for numerous Moak parcels. The Moaks provide an example of Palatines (in this case from Switzerland) marrying into local Dutch families.

5. New York State Library, Manuscripts and Special Collections, Map 74742 (1800–1810, sections 1,2,3), and Van Rensselaer Manor Papers, Ledger A, Part II, 37, 208-216.

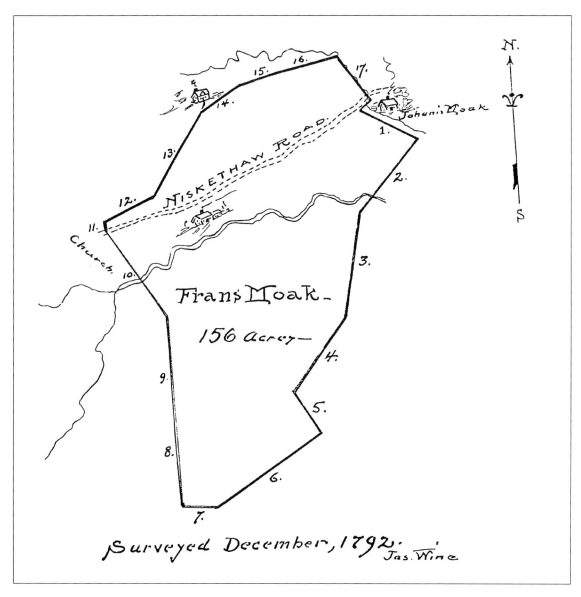

5.12: Three Moak houses are indicated by house symbols on this 1792 survey of the farm of Frans Moak. The house of Johannes Moak (the Moak-Herber House) is at upper right. The Moak-Leedings House on an adjoining farm is indicated at top, center, near the number 14. The house shown on the farm of Frans Moak was in the center of present Feura Bush. Albany County Hall of Records, *Book 17, Farm Maps and Surveys,* page 80.

Construction: The house was in two sections—a stone addition and a frame section, both under the same roof. Catherine Herber, a descendant, was told by her grandfather that the wooden house, the larger half, was the older part. A shed wing housing kitchens was added across the two sections. Only the view of the kitchen wing was included with the Polgreen photos; the photograph shows a chimney at each end of the main house in addition to two kitchen chimneys.

THE MOAK-LEEDINGS HOUSE

Location: The house stands on the west side of Route 32, at the end of a lane behind a convenience store, in the hamlet of Feura Bush, Albany County.

History: A farm owned by Christopher Moak was located on the Onesquethaw Road at present Feura Bush. A Bleecker farm survey of September 17, 1776, shows that land was taken from Christopher's farm for Henry Moak. According to surveys of the 1790s, the farms of Christopher Moak and Henry Moak adjoined. The stone Moak-Leedings House was, by tradition, the home of the Christopher Moak family. In 1807, Henry Moak, Jr., the son of Henry Moak and Elizabeth Heller, leased the farm from patroon Stephen Van Rensselaer. Henry married Lucy Brate in 1813. After his death in 1820, she married John Leedings; their descendants lived in the stone house for five generations. (Waldron Mosher Polgreen may have found a connection between the Moshers, his relatives, and the Leedings family, which led him to this house.) As with the Moak-Herber House, the railroad took some of the Moak-Leedings farm in 1865, and the Selkirk railroad yards took more in 1926. Other acreage was taken by the Owens-Corning Company for a fiberglass manufacturing plant in 1971. Fortunately, the house has survived.

Construction: The stone house, dating probably to the 1790s, is constructed of coursed limestone blocks. The house has exposed first-floor beams and a horizontally divided front door. It is an example of a story-and-a-half farmhouse

5.13: The coursed stones of the Moak-Leedings House were deliberately laid in graduated rows, with the smaller ones at the top. This sometimes was done with the clapboards on houses showing New England influence, and was an optical illusion intended to make the building look taller. The doorway is flanked with small, double-hung windows.

with Federal-style detailing, a type popular into the first decade of the nineteenth century. (See, for example, the Slingerland-Winne House.)

The Moak-Leedings House has a central hall, under which there is cross-framing in the cellar. A parlor on the left side of the hall retains a Federal-style mantel with dentil molding, while the room opposite has a plain mantel in Federal style with a matching cupboard. Deep but narrow planed beams (eleven inches by five inches) are exposed in the first-floor rooms. The jambed fireplaces are supported by stone piers in the cellar. The date *1809* stippled on a stone at the corner of the house by the barn may refer to the date of the barn's construction.

A picture window has been installed on the left front of the house since the photo was taken, and the barn shown at left is gone.

THE HENRY SLINGERLAND-WINNE HOUSE

Location: The house is on Winne Lane, off Route 32, on the Onesquethaw Creek, southwest of Feura Bush.

History: Teunis Slingerland, who occupied the Teunis Slingerland House (page 72), had two children who later built stone houses for their own families. One of the sons, Henry Slingerland, born in 1765, and his wife, Eve Vanderzee, born in 1766, built their house across the fields south of his father's home. A stone over the front entrance with his initials, *HSL*, and the date *1806*, gives the year of construction. Their daughter, Nellie M. Slingerland, and her husband, Leroy Winne, inherited the property. A Winne descendant now lives in the house, the seventh generation of the Slingerland-Winne family to reside there.

Construction: The house, of roughly coursed fieldstone, reflects the evolution away from authentic Dutch construction. The house plan features a center hall; Federal-style fireplaces with jambs are located at each end of the house.

5.14: This view looks east across the fields along Winne Lane. The dead-end lane, east of the Henry Slingerland-Winne House, is part of an old road that once continued through to the present Onesquethaw Creek Road.

5.15: Only one photograph of the Slingerland-Winne House was included with the Polgreen photos. A rear view, it shows the original house in the middle of the picture, with a stone wing, at left. On the right is a separate summer kitchen, with a tall chimney and a bake-oven. The protruding oven is protected by a low shingled roof near the rear corner of the kitchen.

THE ABRAHAM OSTRANDER HOUSE

Location: The house, now gone, was on Brookview Station Road, east of Brookview, in Schodack, Rensselaer County.

History: The farm and house of Abraham Ostrander were indicated on a map drawn by John E. Van Alen, showing Schodack farm surveys of 1787-1788. In addition, a house at this location, although not identified by name, was suggested on Bleeker's 1767 map. According to a cellar cornerstone in the house, which was recorded in 1940, the original part of the house was built in 1765. The stone read *Anno 1765 E/A Os* [6] (for Abraham Ostrander, who was born in 1723, the son of Teunis Ostrander of Ulster County, and his cousin, Elizabeth, to whom he was married in 1753). After Abraham Ostrander died in 1811, Ostrander descendants occupied the house through the nineteenth century. Situated on the last 140 acres of the Ostrander farm, the house survived into the 1940s.

Construction: The house was the only all-frame structure Polgreen photographed. It can be surmised that he did not think the appearance of the early-nineteenth-century, two-story front part was Dutch. He probably looked at the cornerstone, which identified the builder. Polgreen had some Ostrander ancestors and may have been interested in the site for that reason. A current resident of the farm believes that the cornerstone was part of the rear foundation, suggesting the rear wing was the original house of Abraham and Elizabeth Ostrander. The flush roof (without any overhang) of the wing, and the fact it had its own cellar, indicate it was an early building.

The small frame wing, although old, provides a visible contrast with the earlier Dutch-style houses, such as the Van Wie or Bries Houses. The roof is less steep and the windows are double-hung sash. This type of small, probably one-room frame house was common among settlers arriving in the Albany region shortly before the Revolution.

6. Photo and notation, June, 1940 by "M.G.W." from the files of the Historical Society of Esquatak, Schodack, NY.

5.16: The two-story frame Abraham Ostrander House, c.1800–1820, lacks symmetry, suggesting the front section is an addition. Some small-paned, twelve-over-eight windows have survived from the early nineteenth century.

5.17: The gable end, at right, reveals nogging (wall filling) of unmortared bricks, common in the nineteenth century.

5.18: This photograph gives a clear view of the story-and-a-half rear wing. It is probable that this "wing" was the original 1765 house. Windows have been replaced. A shed, painted white, has been added to cover an entrance to the cellar. The cornerstone dating the house was visible within this entrance.

AFTERWORD

It is a tribute to the family of Waldron Polgreen that his invaluable pictures of old houses near Albany were preserved for over sixty years. The Polgreen photographs preserve views of buildings whose original construction dates ranged from the late-seventeenth century to the early-nineteenth century. His detailed pictures provide information on houses since demolished and give some insight into the deplorable state of historic preservation around Albany during the Depression years of the 1930s and 1940s.

At the end of the seventeenth century and in the beginning of the eighteenth, the area around Albany still had close ties to its Dutch heritage; residents built farmhouses that had recognizable connections with the North European homelands of their parents and grandparents. The earliest houses shown in the Polgreen photos, such as those of the Staats, Coeymans, Van Wie, Bronck and Bries families, with their jambless fireplaces, steep roofs, shutters, and casement windows, could have been transported to the Netherlands without causing a stir there. Probably they would have been noted only because they had deep cellars.

An early-eighteenth-century house with gable-end parapet walls and open fireplaces—like the Hendrick Bries House—was an echo of the Hudson Valley connection to a Dutch past. Such houses were built through the 1740s, but only rarely later. The new gambrel-roofed houses built in the 1750s and 1760s by younger members of some of these same families reflected a change that was deeper than mere architectural style. The Dutch enclaves around Albany were moving toward amalgamation with other elements of the population. New ideas about convenience, privacy, space and heat would alter the face of the upper Hudson Valley.

The gambrel-roofed houses showed the influence of outside styles, adopted through contact with English colonists on Long Island, in New Jersey, and along the lower Hudson River. The local gambrel-roofed houses, however, also retained many of the architectural features of their Dutch-style predecessors.

In a parallel development, as the English influence grew in the Albany area, a structure such as the Van Sante-Bleecker House echoed the fortified Georgian-style country houses built along the Mohawk River by Sir William Johnson and other landowners.

Despite these stylistic changes, however, the past was not gone. The similarities between gambrel-roofed houses confirmed a clannishness among their owners. The story-and-a-half gambrel-roofed houses, in their resemblance to each other and to the neighboring older Dutch-style dwellings, reaffirmed their owners' status as part of the Dutch community. The intricate webs of family, religion and language still existed. In light of this continuing Dutch influence and the carry-over of architectural features, the gambrel-roofed houses can legitimately be considered a stage in the evolution of Dutch housing forms in the upper Hudson Valley.

The Revolutionary War, however, was an ideological event too large to ignore. To be part of the new American society, with its endless possibilities for progress, was too tempting to resist. Dutch associations, already weakened, were abandoned. Massive population growth in the Albany area blurred old connections, and architecture became standardized over wider areas as fashionable styles caught popular fancy.

Though today popularly considered an "old Dutch house," the stone Moak-Leedings House of the 1790s, for example, has little in common with the Dutch-style houses of a half-century earlier. Gone are the steep roofs, casement windows, colored shutters, Dutch hinges, open fireplaces and built-in beds which gave a regional flavor to houses in the Hudson Valley. A late-eighteenth-century farmhouse such as the Moak-Leedings House was instead a link in the evolution away from Dutch housing patterns near Albany. With its Federal-style center hall, decorative stair, jambed fireplaces, use of second-floor space, and adoption of popular molding styles emanating from Boston, it reflected contacts with New England and a new diversity of population.

The seventeen houses photographed by Waldron Polgreen span a century of change. They range from regional dwellings with North European medieval origins to gambrel-roofed houses reflecting English architectural influence, and finally include houses borrowing popular building styles with little regional identity. The changing house styles marked the stages of the transition of area residents. Gradually, the up-river area emerged from an ethnic enclave at the beginning of the eighteenth century to the cosmopolitan society that characterized the region by 1800.

SUGGESTED READINGS

Recommended sources on the subject of Dutch-style architecture in the Hudson Valley include the following:

Remembrance of Patria: Dutch Arts and Culture in Colonial America, 1609–1776, by Roderic H. Blackburn and Ruth Piwonka (Albany: Albany Institute of History and Art, 1988). This comprehensive resource depicts Hudson Valley Dutch paintings and artifacts, and includes encyclopedic text on urban and rural life.

Dutch by Design: Tradition and Change in Two Historic Brooklyn Houses, by Kevin L. Stayton (New York: Universe, 1990). An in-depth study of two houses tells how they were moved to the Brooklyn Museum.

"Early Albany: Buildings before 1790," by Paul R. Huey, in *Albany Architecture: A Guide to the City*, edited by Diana S. Waite (Albany: Mt. Ida Press, 1993). The chapter deals with Dutch houses in the City of Albany.

Dutch Houses in the Hudson Valley Before 1776, by Helen Wilkinson Reynolds (New York: Payson and Clarke, 1929; reprinted Dover, 1965). Prepared under the auspices of the Holland Society, this survey of surviving houses has been the old-house-buff's handbook.

Pre-Revolutionary Dutch Houses and Families in Northern New Jersey and Southern New York, by Rosalie Fellows Bailey (New York: William Morrow, 1936; reprinted Dover, 1968). Prepared under the auspices of the Holland Society, the book presents invaluable photographs of early houses, as well as research.

Peter Kalm's Travels in North America: The English Version, by Peter Kalm, edited by Adolph B. Benson (New York: Dover, 1966). The writer, a Swedish naturalist, describes the environs of Albany and explains local construction methods in 1749.

New World Dutch Studies: Dutch Arts and Culture in Colonial America, 1609-1776, edited by Roderic H. Blackburn and Nancy A. Kelley (Albany: Albany Institute of History and Art, 1987). The essays deal with Dutch arts and culture in colonial America.

New Netherland Studies, An Inventory of Current Research and Approaches, "Bulletin Knob," Jaargang 84, Number 2/3, June 1985. The journal in Dutch and English features analysis of Dutch-style houses based on building contracts.

The Old Dutch Homesteads of Brooklyn (Long Island Historical Society, 1985). This exhibition brochure contains pictures of Dutch-style houses and a brief but useful text.

The People's Choice: A History of Albany County in Art and Architecture, by Allison P. Bennett (Albany: Albany County Historical Association, 1980; reprinted Purple Mountain Press, 1995). The book provides valuable illustrations of paintings and early houses as well as information on the area's Dutch heritage.

The New World Dutch Barn: A Study of Its Characteristics, Its Structural Systems, and Its Probable Erectional Procedures, by John Fitchen (Syracuse: Syracuse University Press, 1968). This is the standard book locating and explaining the construction of the unique barns found in areas of early Dutch settlement.

Dutch Barns of New York: An Introduction, by Vincent J. Schaefer (Fleischmanns, N.Y.: Purple Mountain Press, 1994). The basics of Dutch barn construction are featured in this well-illustrated book.

ILLUSTRATION INDEX

SUBJECT INDEX

THE AUTHORS

SHIRLEY W. DUNN has given classes and lectures on the topics of historic houses, local history, and the Mohican Indians, and has contributed many articles to periodicals. She has worked as a teacher, historic preservation consultant, and at Crailo State Historic Site, a museum of the Dutch. One of the founders of the Dutch Barn Preservation Society, she was first editor of its newsletter. Her book, *The Mohicans and Their Land, 1609–1730*, published in 1994 by Purple Mountain Press, describes the experience of the Mohican Indians with the Dutch.

ALLISON P. BENNETT, historian of the town of Bethlehem for eight years, has written numerous travel and historical articles for newspapers and local historical journals, and has lectured on historical subjects to many organizations in the Albany region. She has published four books: *The People's Choice: A History of Albany County in Art and Architecture*, (1980), reprinted by Purple Mountain Press in 1995; *A History of the Town of Bethlehem NY*, (1968); *Times Remembered*, (1984); and *More Times Remembered*, (1987).

This book is set entirely in Janson, a typeface designed by Miklós Kis. Though he was Hungarian, Kis spent most of the 1680s in Amsterdam and is considered a significant figure in seventeenth-century Dutch typography. This typeface is sometimes erroneously ascribed to the Dutch typecutter Anton Janson, after whom it is named. The version used here is from the font library of Linotype-Hell AG, and is based on the Kis originals.

DESIGNED AND TYPESET BY JERRY NOVESKY